The Word Made Alive

The Pastoral Writings

Of

Bishop Peter Elder Hickman

The Word Made Alive

The Pastoral Writings Of
Bishop Peter Elder Hickman

Published By:

ABM Publications
A division of Andrew Bills Ministries, Inc.
PO Box 6811, Orange, CA 92863

www.abmpublications.com

ISBN: 978-1-931820-29-5

Dedication

To my dearly beloved wife, Mirella, who remains my closest companion in Christ and who is a constant source of inspiration and wisdom for me.

Table Of Contents

BISHOP PETER ELDER HICKMAN

Introduction

You hold in your hands a collection of pastoral writings that were composed over a period of twenty-five years.

Although there is much theology in its contents these writings are primarily pastoral. To say that they are pastoral I mean that they are designed to meet pastoral situations in the life of a local church community. Therefore this is not a comprehensive systematic theological work. Rather, these are writings designed to address pastoral and ministerial needs and are primarily concerned with the edification of the average believer who is trying to integrate the truth of the Gospel of Jesus into one's life.

I must acknowledge my deep indebtedness to my dear friend, Father James Michael Farris, without whom these things would have never been put to writing. Indeed, much of what is written herein comes from him.

I also am indebted to the Rev. Andrew Bills who encouraged me to publish these pastoral writings for the edification of a wider audience throughout the Body of Christ.

But most of all I dedicate this small book to my dearly beloved wife, Mirella, who remains my closest companion in Christ and who is a constant source of inspiration and wisdom for me.

Bishop Peter E. Hickman
Saint Matthew Ecumenical Catholic Church

BISHOP PETER ELDER HICKMAN

Chapter 1

A Way of Being Catholic in Today's World

Introduction

The present day Saint Matthew Ecumenical Catholic Church of Orange, California was founded in November of 1985 under the name of Saint Matthew Old Catholic Mission Church of Orange County. The purpose of the Saint Matthew Mission was to provide a home for the many Roman Catholics who had been marginalized by their own church due to some impediment preventing such persons from participating fully in the sacramental life and ministry of the Roman Catholic Church. The most common impediment was and still remains that of divorce and remarriage without the required ecclesiastical annulment. Since the Saint Matthew Mission was Old Catholic and as such independent of the jurisdiction of the local Roman Catholic diocese I was not prevented from welcoming such Roman Catholics into the full sacramental life of the Old Catholic Church of which I had been ordained a priest. Most of the Roman Catholics who had found their way to the Saint Matthew Mission had never heard that there was such a thing as the Old Catholic Church. So this work was to provide that explanation. For many years this article was published in small booklet form with a blue cover and for a long time was referred to as the "Blue Booklet." However, the actual title of the booklet was A Way of Being Catholic in Today's World.

<u>Saint Matthew Old Catholic Mission Church</u>

Saint Matthew Mission is a Christian community that is

committed to the person of Jesus Christ and to His teaching. We accept and believe the testimony of His apostles who were His first disciples and the eye witnesses of His life, death , and His resurrection from the dead. It was these same disciples that passed on to the Church their own testimony about the person of Jesus and the events of His life. Embodied in their testimony are the very teachings of Jesus Himself.

The Apostolic Tradition and the Gospel

We call this testimony of the first disciples the Apostolic Tradition. The word "tradition" means that which is passed on from one generation to the another. The first disciples, whom we call apostles (meaning "one who is sent"), proclaimed (kerygma= proclamation) and taught the message of Jesus which is called the Gospel, (evangel) which means "the Good News." Those who believed in the Good News were baptized and brought into a new community (koinonia= fellowship) that had been formed by these same apostles. This new community was called the Church (ekklesia= the gathered ones). Within this community the Christians, as they came to be called, worshipped together, worked together, and took care of one another. They made every effort to follow the command of Jesus to love one another.

The Apostles entrusted to this new community of faith their testimony, the Apostolic Tradition, to be passed on to succeeding generations. It was their desire that the newly formed Church would not forget this tradition. As Saint Paul the Apostle writes, "So then, brothers and sisters, stand firm and hold to the traditions we passed on to you, whether by word of mouth or by written letter." The Apostolic Tradition was passed on in the written letters and memoirs of the Apostles, which were later collected and preserved into what we now call the New Testament. The Apostolic Tradition was also passed on by "word of mouth." This "oral tradition" is to be found in the continuing life of the Christian community of the Church especially in the Holy Liturgy, that is the Mass, and in the celebration of the sacraments which embody both the written and oral traditions of the Apostles.

The Holy Spirit

Within the Christian community people experience the very presence of God. This immediate presence of God was known as the Holy Spirit. It was the Holy Spirit who empowered the Apostles and others so that they could continue the saving work of Jesus in healing the sick and bring forgiveness of sins. Without the Holy Spirit there could not be an authentic Christian community. The Church came into being when the Holy Spirit came upon the disciples of Jesus at the feast of Pentecost in Jerusalem fifty days after Jesus was raised from the dead.

The Catholic Church

With the passing of time the message of Jesus spread and the life of the Church grew. Very early on the Church came to be called the Catholic Church. The word "catholic" means universal. What Christians meant when they used the term "catholic" was that the Church of Jesus Christ was universal - that the Church embodied those Christians who lived in Rome or Antioch, Alexandria or Ephesus, as well as those who lived in Jerusalem. It also meant that the Church includes those Christians of the past as well as those of the present. As Saint Vincent of Lerins wrote in the fifth century, "in the <u>Catholic Church</u> itself, all possible care must be taken, that we hold that <u>faith</u> which has been <u>believed</u> everywhere, always, by all. For that is <u>truly</u> and in the strictest sense <u>Catholic</u>, which, as the name itself and the reason of the thing declare, comprehends all universally. This rule we shall observe if we follow universality, antiquity, and consent. We shall follow universality if we confess that one <u>faith</u> to be <u>true</u>, which the whole <u>Church</u> throughout the world confesses." In other words, the community founded by the Apostles is one and continuous in both space and time.

The Catholic Church Splits in Two

By the time the Catholic Church was about 1000 years old, disagreements among Christians of the East and Christians of the West caused the Church to virtually split in half. Where there was once only one Church now, in the year 1054, there seemed to exist two Churches. Earlier, smaller breaks in the Church had occurred including the Nestorian Church of the East as well as the Coptic (Egyptian) Church. But the Schism of 1054 between the Greeks and the Latins marked the deepest split ever . Each half of the Church claimed to be the One, True, Catholic, and Apostolic Church. They even went so far as to excommunicate one another. Today the Eastern Church is known as the Orthodox Church and the Western Church became known as the Roman Catholic Church.

The leaders of the Orthodox Church were called patriarchs. There were four Patriarchates in the East: Constantinople, Alexandria, Jerusalem, and Antioch. The Roman Catholic Church was led by the bishop of Rome who is called the Pope. The leader of the Coptic Church is also called by the title "Pope." The head of the Nestorian Church of the East is called a "katholikos" and this is a title that is used by the Armenian Church for their leader as well.

The Issues of Church Leadership and Authority

One of the major disagreements that caused the rift between the East and the West was the issue of Church leadership and authority. Jesus had commissioned His apostles to be the first leaders of the Church. Before the Apostles died they appointed others to lead the Church for the next generation. These leaders were called bishops (episkopas/overseers).

This appointment became a sacramental act through the laying on of hands that came to be called ordination or holy orders. The Holy Apostles ordained the first bishops to be their successors in providing leadership and pastoral care for the Christian Church. These first bishops, in turn, ordained others after them. This sacred line of leadership extending all the way back to Jesus Christ is called the Apostolic Succession.

As the Church continued to grow and develop through the centuries, some bishops became more powerful and more esteemed than others. The bishop in the Church of the City of Rome had considerably more influence over the bishops of smaller churches in other areas. It was not long until the bishops of Rome, the Popes, began to insist that they had direct authority over all other bishops and the entire Catholic Church.

Many bishops, particularly of the eastern part of the Church, resisted this claim of the Roman bishops. The final outcome of this dispute was the split between the Orthodox Church of the East from the Roman Church of the West called the Great Schism of 1054.

The Reformation

After the Great Schism, the Roman Catholic Church continued to grow and develop throughout Western Europe. For the next 450 years, during the latter Middle Age, the Popes consolidated their power and extended their influence over the Church and society as a whole.

With the dawn of the sixteenth century, the Roman Catholic Church was overcome with both moral and political corruption. Many concerned religious leaders made efforts to reform the Church. These efforts at reform became collectively known as the Reformation. Although most Christians felt the need for a reformation of the Church, they could not agree on the nature and extent of the needed reforms. This resulted in further splits in the Catholic Church. The groups that broke away from the Roman Catholic Church at this time were called Protestants because they "protested" the policies of the Roman Papacy.

The Church Expands

As devastating as the Reformation was to the unity of the Roman Catholic Church, it did not prevent the Church from continuing to grow and develop through many courageous missionary enterprises. Through the great discoveries of European explorers, vast territories all over the world became accessible to missionaries of both the Roman Catholic Church and the various Protestant churches. The Roman Catholic missionaries especially among the Franciscans and Jesuits as well as other monastic orders, brought the Christian Faith to peoples who had never before heard the message of Jesus Christ.

An Independent Catholic Church in Holland

In the early half of the eighteenth century, another dispute arose within the Roman Catholic Church between the Jesuits and another Roman Catholic party called the Jansenists. The Jansenists were driven out of Roman Catholic France by King Louis XIV. They sought refuge in Holland under the protection of the Roman Catholic Archbishop of Utrecht. The Pope intervened on behalf of the Jesuit cause. Contrary to Church law, the Pope deposed the elected Archbishop and sought to appoint a man of his own choosing to become the next Archbishop of Utrecht. The Dutch Royal Family intervened on behalf of the Dutch Catholics by preventing the papal appointee from entering the country. Eventually, bishops elected by the Dutch Catholics were duly consecrated by the Roman Catholic Bishop, Varlet, who was traveling through Holland at this time for Utrecht , Haarlem, and Deventer. Thus, was created an independent Dutch Catholic Church with a sacramental life that is considered valid, though illicit, by the Roman Catholic Church.

Pope Pius IX, Vatican I, and the Dogma of Papal Infallibility

In 1869-70, Pope Pius IX presided over a Church Council that came to be called Vatican I. For centuries the question of authority within the Catholic Church had been debated. Ultimately there were two points of view on the matter: 1) The Conciliarists who believed that the supreme authority within the Church was best expressed through the Ecumenical Council. This meant that even the Pope was subject to the authority of the Ecumenical Council; 2) the Ultra-montanists who believed that the ultimate authority within the Catholic Church is best expressed through the person of the Pope as an absolute monarchy. Pius IX sought to resolve this question once and for all by convening The first Vatican Council in 1869. It was at this council that Pius IX was able to force through the twin notions of the infallibility of the papal teaching office in all matters of faith and morality as well as the idea of the universal primacy or jurisdiction of the Papacy with regard to the governance of the Catholic Church. Papal infallibility and primacy of jurisdiction were proclaimed dogmas of the Roman Catholic Church. Papal Infallibility meant that when the Pope, by virtue of his office as successor to the Apostle Peter, speaks on behalf of the Church in regard to faith and morals, he speaks without error. In other words, it is impossible for the Pope to make a mistake when he speaks ex cathedra (from the chair of Peter) on behalf of the Church. This newly declared dogma of the Church must be believed by every Catholic under pain of sin.

The Old Catholic Movement

Many Catholics, especially in Germany, Austria, and Switzerland, disagreed with the action of pope Pius IX and the first Vatican Council. These dissenting Catholics continued to embrace the conciliarist point of view. They believed that although the Pope may be the leading bishop of the Catholic church, he does not possess the charism of infallibility and universal primacy.

These charisms are reserved only for the Ecumenical Council of which even the Pope is accountable. The infallibility and universal primacy of the Pope is not an authentic Catholic belief nor was it ever a part of the teachings of Jesus Christ or of the ancient apostolic

Tradition. Many of these Catholics who disagreed with Vatican I formed continuing Catholic communities independent of Rome that were called Old Catholic. They were called Old Catholics because they sought to turn the clock back and adhere to the beliefs and practices of the ancient united Catholic Church of the earliest centuries.

These Old Catholic communities then received their Apostolic Succession through the Archbishop of the Independent Dutch Catholic Church in Utrecht. The Archbishops of Utrecht trace their Apostolic Succession all the way back to the Holy Apostles. So the Old Catholics possess a valid line of succession and therefore have a valid priesthood with valid sacraments. This fact is acknowledged by the Roman Catholic Church.

The Old Catholic Movement in England and North America

The Old Catholic movement then spread from the European continent to England when the Archbishop of Utrecht consecrated Arnold Harris Mathew to be bishop for the English Old Catholics at the dawn of the 20th century. Later, Bishop Mathew consecrated an Austrian nobleman, Rudolph Francis Prince de Landas Berghe et de Rache, Duc de Saint Winock (1873-1920) to be an Old Catholic bishop.

With the outbreak of the First World War the "prince bishop" came to the United States, bringing with him the seeds of the Old Catholic Movement to North America.

Other Catholic Communities That Are Not Roman

Old Catholicism is closely related in kind to other Catholic communities that became independent of Rome. These other Catholic communities continue to grow throughout the world. For example, there are presently five million members of the Brazilian Apostolic Catholic Church of Brazil (Durarte Costa). The Philippine Independent Catholic Church (Aglipayan) has over three million members. Other expressions of independent Catholicism exist throughout the USA and the world and are called by various names such as the American Catholic Church, the Western Orthodox Catholic Church, or the churches of the Ecumenical Catholic Communion.

An Authentic Catholic Community

Old Catholics as well as other Catholics who are independent of the jurisdiction of the Church in Rome participate fully in the ancient Catholic tradition and therefore cannot be classified as Protestant. The Protestant churches of today derive from the churches that originally broke away from the Roman Catholic Church during the Reformation of the sixteenth century. The Old Catholic movement is a later historical development of a different kind. To be an authentic Catholic community a group must be able to trace their Apostolic Succession all the way back to the Apostles. That same group must maintain a faithful adherence to the Gospel of Jesus as expressed through the Apostolic Tradition. They must also affirm the Nicene-Constantinopolitan Creed and the teaching of the Ecumenical Councils of the ancient church. Finally , that group must actively participate in the sacramental ministry of the historic Catholic Church.

The communities of the Old Catholic Movement, as well as those communities that derive from the Old Catholics, are authentically Catholic in that they fulfill the abovementioned criteria. One is a Catholic by virtue of one's relationship to the Lord Jesus Christ through the historic Catholic Church. No authority of the Catholic Church can determine whether one is truly Catholic or not simply because that individual in good conscience questions or rejects that authority's leadership.

The Sacramental Ministry

The word "sacrament" is derived from the Latin word sacramentum which is a translation of the Greek word musterion which in English is commonly translated "mystery." A mystery is something that we actually experience but are unable to fully comprehend. A sacrament is a mysterious dynamic moment in which the grace of God is made manifest for the salvation of humanity. The pre-eminent sacrament therefore is the miracle of the incarnation when the eternal Word of God became flesh in the person of Jesus of Nazareth when He was conceived by the Holy Spirit and born of the Blessed Virgin Mary. Jesus is the sacrament of God for the salvation of the world. The Church is the Sacrament of Christ for the world's salvation in that the saving presence of Christ is at work within the community that bears His name. That is why the Church is called the Body of Christ. The sacramental ministry is the work of Christ by means of the Holy Spirit through the Church that brings saving grace to the people of God.

Traditionally, seven sacraments are recognized as normative in the life of the Church: 1) Baptism; 2) Confirmation; 3) Eucharist 4) Reconciliation; 5) Matrimony; 6) holy orders; and 7) Anointing of the sick and dying.

Distinctives of Saint Matthew Mission

How does Saint Matthew Old Catholic mission differ from the Roman Catholic Church? Saint Matthew differs in the following ways:

1) The Catholics of our community do not accept the teaching promulgated by Pius IX and the First Vatican Council concerning papal infallibility and universal primacy. Therefore we are a Catholic Community independent of Roman jurisdiction which means that we are not bound by the guidelines and regulations of the Roman Code of Canon Law.

2) As a result Priests and bishops are free to marry and fully participate in normal family life.

3) Women are invited to fully participate as equals in the ordained ministry of the Catholic Church.

4) The divorced and remarried are not excluded from participating in the full sacramental life of the Church.

5) The use of contraception and artificial insemination are issues of conscience between a husband and wife. The use of contraception in limiting the size of one's family is not considered a sin.

6) Each Catholic is an equal member of the Church. The ordained do not "own" the sacramental ministry of the Church. The celebration of the sacraments and the liturgy belong to the whole people of God. Therefore, the laity play an indispensable role in the ministry and governance of the Church.

7) At Saint Matthew no Christian is excluded from the sacramental ministry of the Church. All baptized Christians, be they Catholic, Protestant, or Orthodox are invited to

participate fully in the worship and sacramental celebrations of our community.

An Invitation

It is my hope that this brief description of the Catholic life and identity of the Saint Matthew Old Catholic Mission will help the reader to better understand where our faith community fits into the history of the Catholic Church. If anyone reading this feels that there would be some benefit from our ministry we are happy to welcome that one into the life of our church. We are pleased to invite any and all to join us in an exciting and historic adventure with the Lord Jesus as we seek to discover a way of being Catholic in today's world.

Chapter 2

A Church for a New Millennium

Introduction

At the close of the twentieth century much had changed in the first fifteen years of my ministry as the pastor of the Saint Matthew Church in Orange , California. From its founding in November of 1985 the congregation had grown from six families to more than one hundred families. With that growth in membership there had also come a growth in our understanding of the radical inclusivity of the Gospel message of Jesus. From the first we understood that the divorced and remarried Catholic needed a place to worship and participate in the sacramental life of the Catholic Church that had been denied them in the Roman Catholic Church. The ministry of Saint Matthew was an effort to reach out to these marginalized people who desired to maintain their Catholic identity and still practice their beloved Catholic faith unhindered by canon laws that would restrict their access to the Church's celebration of the sacraments. But over time we came to realize that there were other good Catholics who had become excluded from the life of the Church. Beside the divorced and remarried there were other groups of persons that were without a church home. These were the married Roman Catholic priests who were shunned because they fell in love and decided to marry their beloved. Of course this meant for them a loss of their active participation as priests in the Roman Catholic Church. These were also women who experienced a call of God to serve as priests but were denied ordination merely because of their gender. Finally, we also became aware of our sisters, brothers, and children who had a homosexual orientation. These were the excluded who must now be welcomed back into the fullness of Catholic life. These are the ones whom the Church must recognize as full members of the Body of Christ and be accepted as God created them to be. They, too, are valued and loved by Christ and must be restored to their rightful place within the inclusive community of the Catholic Church. Perhaps God was using our small Catholic community as a prophetic voice as to what God intended to do with the coming dawn of the third millennium of the Church. The circle of the radical inclusivity of the Gospel was growing bigger even as our vision of what that would mean became ever larger. It was against this background that I wrote the following brief pastoral letter to our faithful just four years after I had been elected and ordained a bishop of the Ecumenical Old Catholic Church.

January 1, 2000
Solemnity of Mary the Mother of God

Dear Sisters and Brothers,

Now we stand at the dawn of the third millennium of the Christian Movement and quite possibly a new era in the history of the church. As we, the small Christian faith communities of The Ecumenical Old Catholic Church, begin this first year of the twenty-first century we stand poised and ready to continue in the noble endeavor that has been entrusted to us by the Holy Spirit.

Up to the present time the Old Catholic Movement has been small and, to some, insignificant. Yet, I am convinced that this will change in the coming century. The power of ideas has been known to change the course of human history. We possess sacred ideals like a bright torch of hope. These very same ideals that we have embraced will ultimately have a lasting impact upon the entire Church of Jesus Christ. This is so because they are rooted in the very teachings of Jesus himself. These ideals are nothing less than the ripening fruit of the Gospel of Christ in our time.

We labor for the living reform of the Catholic Church. Although our efforts for the most part have gone unnoticed by the vast majority of our contemporaries in the larger church of today, I remain convinced that our day is yet to come, and that we are indeed practicing the Catholicism of the future.

We have undertaken to work for justice within the walls of the Church. We are committed to the reform of the Church. We are working for the positive transformation of the Catholic Church. What kind of Church are we looking for?

We believe that the Catholic Church of the future needs to become a compassionate church, fully embracing the truth of the Gospel of Jesus.

We believe that we must become a truly "catholic" church where all are welcome, where the dignity of each is honored, and where everyone is invited to share in the saving work of Christ.

We believe that we must become a truly united church, where the barriers of sectarianism are broken down and the bridges of understanding and cooperation are built.

We believe that we must become a truly ecumenical church, where all the baptized are embraced as one and where common ground is diligently sought with the non-Christian.

Someday, this is what will define what being Catholic really is rather than what organization one officially belongs to; where one is a Catholic by what is within one's heart rather than by what religious group he is a member of; where one is a Catholic by virtue of following the teachings of Jesus, not by the degree of one's conformity to the dictates of a particular church leader.

Let us begin this new millennium with renewed commitment and courage as we together continue in our noble endeavor for the reform and renewal of Christ's church! May the blessing of the Father's grace and the love of Jesus and the wisdom of the Holy Spirit continue to be upon you in this new year of 2000!

The Most Reverend Peter E. Hickman, Bishop, Ecumenical Old Catholic Church

Chapter 3

Marriage and Remarriage in the Church Today

Introduction

Early in 1997 Pope John Paul II issued a moral teaching for Catholic couples who were divorced and had remarried without an ecclesiastical annulment of the first marriage. The second attempt at marriage with someone other than the original spouse was not recognized by the Roman Catholic Church. Yet, in many cases to break up such a subsequent marriage could create unnecessary economic hardship particularly for older couples without the means of maintaining two households in place of the one shared household. The moral teaching of John Paul II would permit such couples to continue living in the same house and continue to share a common life. However, such couples according to this teaching must not participate in any sexual sharing with each other as that would be considered adulterous. So while a couple in such circumstances could live together they were forbidden to engage in sexual sharing with each other. Many of the married couple at Saint Matthew Church were troubled by such teaching because they were divorced from their first spouse and now were in a subsequent marriage with another. To follow this teaching would be a great burden. I was reminded of the words of Jesus to the religious legalists of His day, the Pharisees when He said, "You tie enormous burdens upon others and you do not even lift a finger to help them." This pastoral letter was written to help those couples who were burdened by this latest teaching of Pope John Paul II.

March 10, 1997
The Feast of Saint Marcarius of Jerusalem

To the faithful brothers and sisters in Christ:

Grace and peace to you in our Lord Jesus Christ!

We have always been involved in the work of healing, whether that healing work pertains to relationships or to physical illness. The Lord Jesus made no distinction between these two kinds of healing and we follow in His footsteps. Truly, we are called by our Lord Jesus to bring healing and reconciliation to a broken and divided world!

Recent questions of divorce, remarriage, and sexuality have arisen in the Christian community to which I wish to address as the bishop and spokesperson of our beloved community. These questions address the propriety of remarriage and the active sexual life of remarried persons.

The school of marriage teaches valuable lessons which can be applied to all relationships in life. Sometimes that school provides hard lessons in the painful tragedy of divorce. Divorce is a major trauma for all who experience it, whether we speak of the spouses or the children of a family. While we avoid divorce, we are aware of its reality and ask God to heal our hearts when they have been broken by this reality.

Saint Paul, the apostle, in his epistle to the church at Rome, asks, "Who shall separate us from the love of Christ?" Too often, however, it is the church itself, which provides the answer. At the precise time when we have been broken and made vulnerable by the experience of divorce, our misery is compounded by a sense of condemnation by our Christian church. It is not the healing voice of Jesus we hear, like the Samaritan woman at the well in John's gospel, but rather, it is the voice and weight of canon law and the judgment of church leaders which confront us and add to our grief.

It is apparent that those who have divorced and remarried are still in need of the sacramental life of the Church. We join our Eastern Christian brothers and sisters in an ancient tradition of supporting those who have remarried by counseling them to now reflect upon all that has passed and to grow in all that will come during their new marriage. Such growth can only be successful in union with the sacramental life of the Church and in the Church's teaching on the life of prayer and the excellent way of love as taught in the Holy Scriptures and practiced by faithful families. To deny the gift of sexual union to those who have remarried is to destroy rather than to support the success of a remarried couple. For sexuality is a source and a celebration of love between husband and wife. It is a special and secret place which allows intimate sharing. It is the measure of a healthy relationship between two individuals who are of the age and health to share in this manner. While we recognize that many difficulties can cause the suspension or termination of sexual sharing between husband and wife, we recognize that it is they alone who can make the decision to suspend this part of their relationship, and that no official of the Church should make a blanket declaration of the place of sexuality in the life of married or remarried Christian couples. Indeed, we consider it a possible danger for marriages to be denied sexual sharing. Since such frustration could lead to seeking such comfort from others, out of a misguided intention to conform to the teachings of one's church. Compassionate guidance and loving support are rather the appropriate responses which clergy and laity should offer. For indeed, the strength of the Church depends upon the strength of our families, whether those families are formed by an original marriage or by a subsequent remarriage.

As your bishop, I intend to do all that is possible to support and defend the continued success of all families. Those who are remarried will find equal support from this faith community. Our hope and our dream is that of wiping away every tear with the grace of the risen Christ, and celebrating the love of God as it exists between husband and wife, parent and child, our brothers and sisters of the Christian community, and between all of the human family. Every family is valuable and every marriage deserves support for its emotional, sexual, and economic stability.

May Christ bless us and forgive us our sins of the past. With the knowledge that He does, let us allow Him to complete the work of salvation, by not only administering His forgiveness, but also healing us and filling us with grace, that we may walk in love anew, and discover the path from which we may have previously wandered. May God grant you the love and wisdom of the Holy Spirit as you work to create a happy and healthy life with your spouse and your family!

In Him who is able to understand our weakness and fill us with grace,

The Most Reverend Peter Elder Hickman, bishop
The Diocese of Ecumenical and Old Catholic Churches

Chapter 4

The Sacred Body
A Pastoral Letter on Human Sexuality

Introduction

In 2001 as it became apparent that some other Catholic Intentional Eucharistic Communities were seeking to affiliate with Saint Matthew Church that certain questions regarding human sexuality in the Christian life needed to be addressed in the pastoral care of all those were now making their home among us. Besides the divorced and remarried we were also attracting Catholic priests who had gotten married as well as a number of Gay and Lesbian persons in permanent loving relationships. Because of the great controversy throughout the Christian world at that time regarding the issue of homosexual persons and homosexual relationships, it became necessary to seriously begin to address this issue in light of the radical inclusivity of the Gospel of Christ. I realized that this issue was complicated and difficult to work through. It required much prayerful reflection and study. I soon realized that I needed some help from some very good theological minds. So I formed a committee of theologians and ethicists to assist me in the writing of what could be my most important pastoral letter. Dr. Tony Battaglia, Rev. Dr. James Farris, Sr. Corrine Bailey, Rev. Giovanna Piazza, and others collaborated with me in the writing of this letter. After several drafts and much revision the final text that was published appears in this book. For all the good that is in this text I give credit to those who helped me, for all its shortcomings I take complete and sole responsibility.

Dear Friends in Christ,

1. The reality of the Incarnation is the foundation of this Pastoral Letter.

The sacred body of Christ is a mirror that reflects our own sacred beauty. We experience this beauty each time we gather to celebrate the Eucharist, for we realize that we are what we receive, the Body of Christ. The foundation of our faith is this reality of the Incarnation: that all creation is imbued with the divine presence. We find God in the water, wind, earth and stars, and we find the most profound divine encounter in each other. In our teaching, our celebration, and our actions, we strive to announce Jesus as God's irrevocable —yes to every corner of human history and the striving of every human heart.

The Incarnation of God in Christ is an affirmation of sacredness in all dimensions of human life. The beauty and holiness of all creation is understood from the first chapter of Genesis: God looked at everything that was created and found it to be very good. (Genesis 1:31) And again: They were created, male and female, in the divine image. (Genesis 1:27)

In the New Testament we also find this teaching, which proclaims that ultimately, God will be all in all. (1 Corinthians 15:28) Christian theologians affirm the holiness of the material universe. An example is St. Gregory Nazianzus (4th century), who boldly says, Christ exists in all things that exist. This is the great message of grace: that we and all creation share in the beauty and goodness of God. This includes the life of the body, the life of human love and sexuality, and the life of our sensual experience as a part of the earth. We are one with the earth which exists as our very bodies, and we are one with its rhythms of life, including our experience as sexual beings. This message of creation's sacredness has often been absent in the Church's teaching on sexuality. Therefore, it is necessary to redeem the concept of divinity in all creation, including human sexuality, while holding in dynamic tension the necessity for responsible sexual expression. Such expression is grounded in unselfish love, fidelity, honesty, and commitment; it is neither permissive nor exploitative. We find that there exists a pastoral need to address issues of sexuality in the lives of adults over a lifetime. In this Letter we strongly affirm the goodness of both our human bodies and of a responsible sexual life.

2. Christianity is primarily about love.

The Christian Church is a community gathered in love and gratitude because of God's extravagant gift of love to the whole human family. Our existence as participants in the life of God reveals the meanings of love itself as an outpouring of abundant life. Love is the name that best reveals the essence of God: for God is love. (1 John 4:8) As the Apostle Paul teaches, love is not permissive or self-centered, but is genuinely concerned for the other, e.g.: Love is patient; love is kind; love is not envious or boastful or arrogant...it rejoices in the truth. It bears all things, believes all things, hopes all things, endures all things. Love never ends. Faith, hope, and love abide, these three; and the greatest of these is love. (1 Corinthians 13:4-8, 13)

Such love prompts the Christian community to help one another be faithful to the demands of love. Such love makes the divine mystery present and gives us the measure of our morality. As Paul says, all of the commandments are summed up in this single command:

You must love your neighbor as yourself. (Romans 13:9) The outpouring of God's love is the substance of our faith; love of neighbor is the substance of our morality.

3. The development of doctrine emerges through community reflection.

Just as the mystery of love reveals itself gradually in each individual's life, so too the Christian community is continuously growing in its understanding of the infinite gift of God's self-communication and our call to respond. The full understanding of our Christian tradition did not come to the community of faith whole and complete in the era of the apostles, and is not complete even now. So too, an understanding of God's loving self-communication continues to unfold, even into our own times. We characterize this phenomenon as the development of doctrine; the development of Christian morality. We see this process of development at work even within the community of the first generation of Christians with regard to the question of whether or not Gentiles may be included among the followers of Jesus.

About a decade after the formation of the Christian movement, the apostle Peter realizes the implications of the gospel of Jesus with regard to the inclusion of Gentiles into the Church. In his encounter with the Gentile household of Cornelius he says you must know that it is not lawful for a Jew to associate with Gentiles or to have any dealings with them, but God has made it clear to me that no one should call any person unclean or impure. (Acts 10:28) This story concludes with the revolutionary act of receiving the Gentile household of Cornelius into the Church through baptism and the gift of the Holy Spirit. More recently, the process of the development of doctrine can be clearly seen with regard to the institution of slavery. Nowhere in the writings of the New Testament is there any explicit condemnation of this inhuman practice. For centuries Christians engaged in, and the Church supported, the institution of slavery in various forms. Not until the nineteenth century did the Catholic Church formally condemn this practice. We now consider the institution of slavery to be intrinsically evil and not consistent with the gospel of Christ and Christian faith. This evolution of understanding comes in many ways, but wisdom and moral insight are especially present in the Christian community as it prayerfully reflects on Scripture, tradition, and human experience. Thus, when Church leaders articulate a teaching, their words should give expression to the wisdom of the community. In this way, moral authority is akin to poetry—it speaks of what the faith community already knows and cherishes, but in such a way that these deep treasures emerge with new freshness, power, and clarity in the speaking.

4. We address three specific issues of love and sexuality.

In light of the Incarnation, the call to love, and the development of our understanding of the demands of this love, we address three specific issues that have practical implications for our faith communities: divorce and remarriage, same-sex relationships, and the sexual lives of our clergy. This, by no means, exhausts the range of issues that could be taken up. However, they are issues that require a response from our Church with regard to its policies and practices. There are many other issues of human sexuality that might be considered in a pastoral Letter. These include: persons who are called to lead a celibate life, persons who are without a sexual partner through no choice of their own, the sexual maturation of adolescents, and the nurturing of love in married couples. These topics deserve serious attention, and raise issues of the differences among people and the changes we face as we progress through life. Nevertheless, in this document we limit ourselves to three topics which merit our attention at this time.

A. Divorce and Remarriage

Divorce is a trauma for all who experience it: spouses, children, and others who are close to the family. Therefore, efforts at healing and reconciliation are important and necessary. When the dissolution of a marriage is still the outcome, however, the family involved and the Christian community are called to love and support one another.

This love includes an invitation to those who are divorced and remarried to participate fully in the sacramental and community life of the Church. Love and faithfulness are strengthened by the healing power of friendship in Christ through the activities, study, and prayer life of our communities and celebrated in the Eucharistic meal and all of the sacraments. Many of us, clergy and lay people alike, have experienced the suffering of divorce, and now extend our hands to those who have been bruised by this experience. In this sense we are wounded healers who joyfully welcome the presence of renewed love in our midst.

We join our Orthodox Christian brothers and sisters in an ancient tradition of supporting those who are divorced and remarried by: embracing them in their brokenness and pain; including them fully in the sacramental life of the

Church; counseling them to reflect on all that has passed and to grow with new insight; and encouraging them to reestablish love and commitment in their lives.1

B. Same-Sex Relationships

The issue of same sex relationships is one where Christian understanding has changed over time. In the past century, Christians have begun to rethink many matters related to sexuality and gender equity. For example, our position on issues of birth control, divorce and remarriage, the right of women to education, the ordination of women, and other matters have been reconsidered. After prayerful reflection and consultation with the members of our faith communities, we offer the following considerations regarding our brothers and sisters who are gay and lesbian.

When Christ was asked to name the greatest commandment, he answered: 'You shall love the Lord your God with all your heart, and with all your soul, and with all your mind.' This is the greatest and first commandment. And a second is like it: 'You shall love your neighbor as yourself.' On these two commandments hang all the law and the prophets. (Matthew 22:37-40)

Jesus urges us to love our neighbor without exception. That is what he did, as story after story in the Gospels show. All human activity is, in fact, measured by this standard of love. The Christian understanding of sexual morality, like many other issues in Christian teaching, has developed over time. What remains consistent is the standard of measure, which is love. In order to clarify and contextualize our understanding of same sex relationships in the life of the Church, we have used the great commandment of love to frame this document. We affirm the goodness of creation and the human body in the context of the incarnation of God in Christ, and believe that we are called to respond to God's presence with love for God and for our neighbor. We regard the teaching of Jesus, and of the whole New Testament, as overpoweringly in favor of love of neighbor and concern for the welfare of others. We recognize that in the past whole groups of people, gay and lesbian persons among others, were often compelled to give up personal wellbeing (or even to suffer) on behalf of supposed moral principles. The arguments that led to such sacrifice are not consistent with the gospel of Christ. Therefore, the Christian community must acknowledge that gay and lesbian persons should be accorded the same dignity and freedom that is the gift of our Creator. Some will reply that Jesus —loved the sinner but hated the sin , and that homosexual behavior is condemned in the scriptures. However, many scripture scholars have recently concluded that the biblical writers did not deal with homosexuality as an orientation. This concept, that people are attracted to members of the same sex as a natural psychological condition, was unknown when the sacred texts were written.

In the time of Paul, for example, homosexual behavior was thought of as bad behavior by heterosexuals, rather than as natural behavior by persons attracted to members of the same sex. Biblical passages often read as condemning homosexuality can, and perhaps should, be read as condemnations of violent and exploitative sexual behavior. When particular sexual behaviors, homosexual and heterosexual, were condemned, it was in the context of promiscuous or exploitative actions, not in the context of loving relationships.

In recent times, the psychiatric and psychological communities of the world have concluded that homosexuality is not an aberration of character, but rather a difference due to biological, psychological and cultural factors.

Our enlightenment to such emerging evidence is causing us, as a society, to reevaluate our understanding of homosexuality. This is not unlike our reevaluation of other prejudices in our culture, such as the bias we have had toward ethnic and racial minorities, and the change in our understanding of the opportunities and equal treatment that should be afforded to women.

The community of faith continues to develop its understanding of the truth that the love of God is present in all creation and therefore in every human being irrespective of race, gender or sexual orientation. Love is measured by the fruit of the Spirit which is love, joy, peace, patience, kindness, generosity, faithfulness, gentleness, and self-control. Against such things there is no law. (Galatians 5: 22-23).

The moral issue for Christians is not whether love is homosexual or heterosexual, or on a continuum between these two. The moral issue is the extent to which love is characterized by the fruits of the Spirit. This applies to all people, whatever their sexual orientation, and is the standard by which Christian behavior is evaluated. Therefore, we joyfully welcome gay and lesbian individuals and couples fully into our faith community.

We have been graced by their presence among us, have

seen the fruits of the Spirit in their lives, and have witnessed their dedication to a life of faith and faithfulness. The love we witness in their lives is the manifestation of their determination to live the gospel despite the obstacles that have been placed before them by both church and society. We offer gay and lesbian couples the support given to others in our community. We embrace these couples, welcome them into the household of faith and provide a context in which to live out the Christian ideal of love, fidelity and commitment to one another. In order to strengthen their shared life together in Christ we offer, to those who desire it, the graces of a holy union blessed by the Church.

C. The Sexuality of Ordained Clergy

Fitness for ordained ministry is measured by the standard of biblical love. Like God's grace, the call to ministry is found in persons who are male and female, heterosexual and homosexual, single, widowed, divorced and married. Clergy, in their sacramental and pastoral role in the community, are called to exemplify an extraordinary measure of this biblical love in their ministry and in their lives. This is especially true considering the vulnerability of those who look to them for guidance.

When sexual exploitation is found in the ministry of the Church it is especially damaging both to those persons involved and to the beloved community of faith. Inappropriate and exploitative sexual behavior on the part of clergy is categorically intolerable. When evaluating a person for candidacy and/or continuation as an ordained member of our faith community we look for the qualities of commitment, maturity, insight, and unselfish love. These qualities, and other characteristics of grace-filled ministry, are not limited to persons of a particular gender, sexual orientation or marital status. We joyfully welcome all called and qualified persons to ordained ministry, and we are enriched by the grace of their diversity.

5. Sexuality in a larger context

Not everyone is called to a relationship of sexual intimacy. Some are called only for a time in their lives. Divorce and death end some of our relationships and the sexual sharing that accompanies them. Others choose a celibate life. Still others long for a relationship of loving sexual expression, but never find the appropriate person with whom to join their lives. Sexual expression for some will reflect a season of life, for others the entirety of their adult lives, and for still others it will not be present at all.

As we observe the many varieties of lifestyle in our society and Church, we also recognize that our sexual lives, like all other experiences we share in this life, will end. With this in mind, we are reminded of the limitations of our sexual identities. There is a place and time to encounter God that is beyond sexual and personal distinction, as well as beyond age, ethnicity, and all other things that distinguish us.

6. Conclusion

The life we are called to lead is a challenging one. We are spirits embodied in a material world which is filled with God's presence. Living in that presence is a great joy, and it calls us to be the very best versions of ourselves. It is also true that living according to the ideal of love of neighbor and of God is not only a blessing but also a task which involves faithfulness, self-giving and maturity.

For most of us, that task will also involve finding a partner to whom we can dedicate ourselves and with whom we can live in physical and emotional fidelity. In this quest for a partner and in this life of fidelity, the differences between us, of gender or sexual orientation, are not as important as the ways in which we are the same. For those called to share their life with another in committed partnership, finding the right partner and living with that partner in love is not easy, but can be a life filled with the grace and joy of the Spirit. Centuries of our tradition identify a life of loving commitment and responsible fidelity as the surest path to human happiness. We affirm this reality, and urge all members of our communities to pray for the grace that nurtures and enables such a life.

The many ways in which we are different enrich our community. The personal and psychological differences among us, our individual talents, do this in a clear sense. Other differences, of ethnicity and culture, of age and gender, as well as differences of sexual orientation, also enrich the community. This rich diversity makes it possible to be open to the wonders of the world and of each new day, for every day is different and we are constantly being challenged to celebrate the ways in which life is always changing around us. In this Letter we have considered three areas where people have traditionally disagreed but where the Christian community is coming to greater understanding: divorce and remarriage, same sex relationships and choosing persons for ordained ministry.

We affirm that from the point of view of the Christian, the material world is blessed and that our primary response to this blessing is love of God and love of neighbor. In the Christian vision all behavior, including sexual behavior, is judged by the standard of this love and sexuality, with its concomitant vitality, is transformed as a path to God. This is both a challenge for personal growth and a source of great joy. In summary we affirm that our sexuality, like our body itself, is a grace--a gift where the divine and human meet. This grace knows many modalities: youthful and aging, single and married, heterosexual and homosexual. The moral call of this grace, as with all grace, is to make it a medium where love can flourish. For as St. Paul tells us, faith, hope and love abide, these three; and the greatest of these is love. (1 Corinthians 13:13)

In the love of Christ,
Peter Elder Hickman
Bishop of the Diocese of Ecumenical and Old Catholic
Faith Communities

Chapter 5

The Anguish of Disunity and Separation in the Body of Christ

Introduction

The Pathfinder Ecumenical Catholic Community of the Risen Christ was formed by a former Roman Catholic priest, and Holy Cross Father, Rev. Ned Reidy and a former Glen Mary sister, Kathleen McCarthy. This small Intentional Eucharistic Community had departed from the Roman Catholic Church because of their desire for a more gender inclusive Catholic experience. They joined my diocese in 1999 and consequently I became their new bishop. On Pentecost Sunday in June of 2000 I would ordain Kathy McCarthy to be the first Catholic woman priest among us. This pastoral letter was addressed to the Pathfinder Community in response to a public statement issued by the Bishop of the Roman Catholic Diocese of San Bernardino entitled "Instruction on Old Catholic Groups in the Diocese of San Bernardino". The Pathfinder Community was troubled by this statement and this letter was written to provide comfort and encouragement at a time of pain for this community.

April 25, 2000
The Feast of Saint Mark the Evangelist

My Dear Brothers and Sisters in Christ:

The Ancient Church has experienced the anguish of

41

disunity for centuries. Throughout each era of Christianity, there has been a struggle for power and control over the body of Christ that has included injustice, and often brutality, of one Christian group toward another.

You have now experienced this disunity in a most personal fashion. Your community has been singled out as "separated," and you have been in anguish over the words exchanged in this conflict. Yet the saddest part of this situation is that each side of this conflict is suffering. It is for us to approach this grief with the mind of Christ. It is Christ alone who will re-unite the Church. With the Didache, the ancient "Teaching of the Apostles," we pray, "As grain once scattered on the hillsides was in this broken bread made one, so from the four winds bring Your Church into the Reign of Your Son…"

Our Catholic Tradition is also an experience of disunity. While the Roman Church maintains itself as the sole heir of this Tradition, we point to an even older Christian experience of shared responsibility among the bishops of the Church: the democratic participation of all Christians in the governance of the Church through the election of their bishops; and the tradition of both married and celibate clergy in the Church. Because we cling to this older understanding of Catholicism, we are called "Old Catholics." Our spiritual ancestors sought to re-establish these traditions in 1870, when they formed the Union of Utrecht, in the Netherlands. It is not so much that we have separated ourselves from the Roman Church, but that the Roman Church has yet to complete its own renewal, which was begun in Vatican II, but seems to have come to a halt in recent years.

It is with compassion that we speak of our Roman Catholic

brothers and sisters. They now suffer greatly under the weight so many burdens. The Roman Church is short of clergy, experiences tremendous financial loss from legal proceedings against its priests for sexual misconduct, and is engaged in a great struggle over such issues as the ordination of women and married men, contraception, and the voice of the local community in the daily life of its members. It is just such issues as these which have led many of you to join with this Diocese of Ecumenical and Old Catholic Faith Communities. Your quest for inclusiveness and your thirst for justice in the Church were motivators that called you, not so much to separate, but to join with others who journeyed on this same quest and experienced this same thirst. Ultimately, it is the reconciliation of Christ that will bring us all together in the end. We must await this day in patience, though it may feel like the waiting of the tomb. Do not forget that glory of Christ which broke forth from the tomb in light and joy.

And do not forget to take refuge in Christ. It is Christ who brings "peace beyond understanding." This peace is now necessary if you are to maintain the courage of your actions. Ultimately, we are in error if we ask who is right and wrong in this struggle. We are in grief until the day that all Christians, and all humanity, are united in God. With the words of the New Testament, we proclaim that on that day, God will be "all in all," and "every tear shall be wiped away."

Yet, our "validity" is questioned by some authorities. And we are compelled to discuss the understanding of validity. We can show that we are in an unbroken line of Apostolic Tradition in which all our bishops were ordained by validly ordained bishops who trace their ordinations to the apostles of Christ. We have maintained the Scriptures, the sacraments and the tri-fold ministry of bishop, priest and deacon. We confirm the words of Saint Paul when we say that we "hand on to you what we have received from the Lord" through this Apostolic Tradition.

Yet we differ from our Roman brothers and sisters, in that we do not see the Bishop of Rome as having a claim to infallible teaching authority. Our vision is that of collegial authority with the whole Church as represented by all who hold the office of bishop. We also differ from the understanding that the bishop of Rome has the right to make all decisions on the life of the Church in every local community of Christians, regardless of their own local understanding of the Christian way of life.

The world has questioned its own stand on gender and sexuality. It has moved from a repressive stand, which was threatened by an equal place for women and men, to an emerging acceptance of such a change. The world has affirmed the goodness of sexuality and family life, and has seen this as compatible with service to humanity in the name of God. For this reason, we have asked if such changes are compatible with the heart of the Gospel, and we have answered with a resounding YES! Not only is this compatible, it is now a demand of the Gospel – the demand for justice within the Church.

We have proclaimed, with so many of our fellow Christian denominations, that married men have a right to ordination, as called by their communities. Women, too, have a right to ordination, as called by their communities. Couples have a right to the self-determination of the size of their families. All baptized Christians have the right to share in the table of the Lord – barred only by a refusal to reconcile their own injustices.

As our young men and women experience this affirmation of gender and sexuality in the world – as they equally make choices of career into the occupations of doctor, attorney, teacher, engineer – they must question why gender has disallowed women, and marriage has disallowed many men, from the honor of service as a Catholic priest or deacon. As they experience responsible sexuality and the joy of family life, they may ask why they are not allowed to make their own decisions on the size of their families. As they learn about the acceptance of all people as sisters and brothers, they may ask why some baptized Christians do not have the right to receive the body and blood of Christ, simply because they are not Roman Catholic. They will not ask such questions in the Diocese of Ecumenical and Old Catholic Faith Communities. We join with our Anglican brothers and sisters, as well as many Protestant communities, in the call to renewal in such areas. For too long the Christian church has been lagging behind society in hearing this call for justice and renewal. While others may incorrectly question our "validity," we may respond by questioning their fidelity to the message of Christ in the constant renewal of the Church; their sense of justice in the face of inadequate theology that seeks to shore up the status quo; and their charity, which seems absent in terms of creating more harmony within the entire Christian Church.

We do not blame individual bishops, priests, or canon lawyers for the harshness that is often felt in official letters and statements. It is important to remember that we are all members of very fallible organizations, which often sweep us into "an official stance."

Let us endeavor to stand with the heart of Christ. This courageous heart sought always to encounter each individual as a person: a prostitute was seen as a woman, a Pharisee was seen as a troubled seeker, a Samaritan was seen as a victimized human. We are challenged to see past the "official roles" and to call again to our fellow Christians – who bear titles and hold offices – but may themselves be suffering under the weight of policies that bring more anguish and disunity.

We pray "that all may be one." We pray that prayer of Christ that we may some day maintain a oneness like that of Christ and the Father. Until that day, we must speak the truth with a prophetic voice that calls for justice, but we must also reach out with a hand to those who may hear the cry for justice, yet may feel powerless to claim it for themselves and for their people.

The Spirit alone can loosen these paralyzing conflicts which keep the Church as wrapped as Lazarus in the tomb in his bindings of death. For we were meant for more than internal squabbles of "validity." The presence of Christ seems so absent, even in the most "valid" of Eucharistic celebrations, when love is absent.

There is, perhaps, a better way to express the "valid" presence of Christ in the sacramental actions of the Church. We urge you to find that way through prayer and dialog with our fellow Catholics – of all ecclesial connections – so that it may bring harmony and peace to the whole and entire Church. Then we shall be moved by the Spirit to stand with Christ, and respond to our true calling – best expressed in the fourth chapter of Luke's Gospel:

"...to bring glad tidings to the poor, to proclaim liberty to captives, recovery of sight to the blind and release to prisoners; to announce a year of favor from the Lord."

In the Hope of Christ,

The Most Reverend Peter Elder Hickman
Bishop of the Diocese of Ecumenical Old Catholic Communities

Chapter 6

The Life of Prayer and Meditation

Introduction

Next to my wife, Mirella, Father James M. Farris has been my closest friend and companion in ministry throughout my pastoral career. Many are the conversations that we have shared these past almost thirty years concerning theology and the spiritual life. No one has had a greater influence on my spiritual and theological development. Jim Farris has truly been my aman cara, soul friend, in the long faith journey of my life. Genuine spirituality has always been at the center of our interests. It has always been our hope that we would be able to make some small contribution to the spiritual life of those in our pastoral care. Spiritual experience which is the encounter of the human spirit with the Divine Spirit is the greatest longing of the human heart. Both Jim Farris and I are convinced of this. The following letter is the fruit of some of our conversations and really captures the thought of my friend concerning the spiritual life as we understood it back in the Lent of 2000.

March 19, 2000
The Feast of Saint Joseph

Dear Brothers and Sisters in Christ,

The life of prayer and meditation is at the heart of the life of the Christian and the Christian community. The Creed we profess each Sunday at liturgy proclaims that we believe in "all that is seen and unseen." It is the unseen quality of God's love that calls us to prayer. Like the values of Love, Freedom or Meaning – our life in God is not visible to the eye, but bears a reality that guides our hearts as the center of what we are.

It is our sincere desire that we begin a deepening of the life of prayer in each community of the diocese, that we "may be able to grasp fully... the breadth and length and height and depth of Christ's love." (Ephesians 3,18)

The life of personal prayer and meditation is one that gives each of us a strong center for our faith, during busy days and overcrowded schedules. Prayer is the way we call upon God for strength and guidance through the concerns of the day – in both intercession and thanksgiving. Meditation is the path of silence in which we hear God's voice and feel awakened in God's love. St. Paul reminds us of "the mystery of Christ in you, your hope of glory." (Colossians 1, 27) We realize this truth, of our life hidden in God, through prayer and meditation.

Those who seek peace through the religions of both the East and the West proclaim the conviction that there are three paths to God:

The path of adoration, in which we move our consciousness from self to oneness with God – as celebrated in the liturgy and individual devotions.

The path of service to others, especially the marginalized people of the earth.

The path of meditative prayer – which Eastern Christians call "divinization" - since it calls us to understand our participation with Christ in the life of the Blessed Trinity, "in whom we live and move and have our being." (Acts 17,

28) It is our sharing in the very life of God.

In the light of Christ we find that these three paths are really one, for in prayer and mediation we develop compassion for others as we understand that we are all one in Christ. In service to others we come to realize the need for prayer as the source of the love we hope to share and the place of guidance for everyday life. When we realize the unity of all things in God and we understand that each of us is one with the divine, our hearts go out to others for we feel their pain as our own and their joy as well.

Too often in the past the Christian Church has been like Martha in the Gospel of Luke – busy about the details of our religious experience. Jesus reminds us that "only one thing is required": that we sit with Martha's sister, Mary, at the feet of Jesus and listen to his words. Through prayer and meditation we fulfill this admonition of Jesus. Soon I hope to aid the clergy and lay leaders of our parishes in providing opportunities to learn more about prayer and mediation. Hopefully, the spiritual life of our communities will flourish through classes, programs, and retreats on this life of prayer.

The path of spirituality is one that has often been considered the area of "saints" or of those in religious orders. This is a mistaken notion, however, for every Christian is called to the experience of the Divine in the life of prayer and the silence of meditation. Too often, Christians are disappointed in the lack of such experience in their own church communities and feel compelled to seek their spiritual fulfillment in the teachings of other religions. Such experiences of the mystical life are not contrary to our Christian faith, but the fact that Christians must find such experiences outside the rich Catholic tradition must cause us to reflect on our shortcomings as a Christian Church in not meeting such needs. We hope that those who find serenity in their experiences outside our Christian tradition will return to us to share their treasures. Moreover, we hope that the peace that they have

found may find its completion in the beauty of Christ, the fullness of his Wisdom, and the love of their brothers and sisters in the Christian community.

We bless and thank our Jewish brothers and sisters for bequeathing their gift of a living faith to the Christian world. For the Lord Jesus was a Jew and lived in the tradition of Abraham and Sara, Moses and Miriam – who were his ancestors. So, too, we stand with the Moslem community in affirming the oneness of God, who exists in that oneness in every human heart, as well as in every moment and place of the Divine creation. Also, our fellow seekers of the spiritual life in the traditions of India have sought the light of Wisdom through devotion and meditation. Such devotion found a pinnacle of this light in the teachings of the Buddha and in the life of those who follow his teachings. We join with all our fellow humans who seek such Truth and Peace.

But, as Christians, we see the fulfillment of all such human desire in the revelation of Christ. For Christ has manifested to us the truth that lies hidden in the center of each atomic particle as well as the center of every human soul. For those who believe, death is seen as an opening to eternal life. For those who believe, the dying to self in everyday life is an opening to finding God here and now, long before physical death completes our journey to the

Divine. It is our rich Catholic and Christian tradition that teaches us how to lose the self in order to find the true self in Christ (Matthew 10:39). This tradition includes the teaching of many saints and many practices to lead each Christian to such realization of the fullness of Christ. These include the use of the "Jesus Prayer" (also called the prayer of the heart), the rosary, meditation and contemplation, and meditative use of the Scripture. Such great saints as Teresa of Avila and John of the Cross, as well as modern teachers, such as Thomas Merton or Father Basil Pennington and Father Thomas Keating (who teach "Centering Prayer") also provide paths for the spiritual life to the Christian Community.

For so long the people of our diocese have proclaimed each Sunday "All Are Welcome." This phrase has stated that we are a Church known for accepting all people to the table of the Lord. No one is excluded because we respect the dignity of every person. Women are not excluded from the ordained ministry. This has been so important that we have used this phrase on my Bishop's crest, which appears on official documents. Yet, our hope is that this will not be the only hallmark of our Ecumenical Catholic Diocese.

Our desire is that our growth will also be marked by an interior development that matches our external growth in numbers. To be known as a Church that promotes and practices the spiritual life is to be known as followers of the Living Christ and to be the presence of Christ in the world today. As Jesus loved God with the whole of his soul, mind, and strength, so, too, others will see this kind of love in us if we first devote ourselves to the life of prayer that identifies us with Christ and the silence of meditation in which we encounter the Holy One.

As your bishop, I join Saint Paul, in his letter to the Ephesians, as "I kneel before the Father from whom every family in heaven and on earth takes its name; and I pray that he will bestow on you gifts in keeping with the riches of his glory." May the riches of the life of prayer benefit each of us and conform us more closely to the image of Christ!

In the bond of Christ's love,

The Most Reverend Peter Elder Hickman
Bishop of the Diocese of Ecumenical Catholic
Communities

Chapter 7

The Story of Mary

Introduction

Marian devotion is one of the best known characteristics of Catholic spirituality and practice. As a convert to Catholicism from Evangelical Christianity I found the devotion to the Blessed Virgin Mary to be somewhat foreign to my experience and one of the most difficult challenges in becoming fully Catholic. But as time went on I came to deeply appreciate this feature of Catholic life. This happened over time when I gradually realized that not only was Mary the mother of our Lord but that she was through her divine Son the mother of the Church. Then it came to me that since I am an adopted brother of Jesus so I am an adopted child of Mary. Call me a sentimentalist but I have come to love our Blessed Mother and to feel her presence in my life. I am a member of the Rosary Prayer Group at Saint Matthew Church and I look forward to our weekly recitation of the prayer of the Rosary and have found my own Marian devotion to be a truly enriching part of my relationship with her Son , Jesus. This letter was written to bring a greater appreciation of our Lord's mother and her role in God's plan of salvation for the whole world.

March 25, 2008
The Feast of the Annunciation

My Dear Sisters and Brothers,

The story of Mary, the Mother of Jesus Christ, begins as the story of a young Jewish girl in ancient Palestine – a girl of whom we know relatively little. Yet, this story has become a brilliant light of hope and liberation for countless generations around the world. We find a mirror for each one of us in the very simplicity of her life. In the eyes of the world Mary achieved no great historical deeds, and rose to no positions of importance in her day. In this, she is like most of us – caring for our families, working at the tasks of each day, and praying for the ones we love. It is precisely in this simplicity that Mary reflects a sense of courage and faith – a sense of the divine presence that transformed her life at its core.

We recognize her connection to us in the troubles of her young life. Though our Catholic tradition honors her as the Blessed Virgin Mary, the scriptures tell a story of a young betrothed woman of faith, faced with a pre-marriage pregnancy, misunderstanding, and the scrutiny of others. She is loved nevertheless by her fiancé, Joseph the Carpenter. The story continues with the trials of the newly married couple facing homelessness, then political persecution as they flee from their homeland. It is also a story of immigrants who must live as "strangers in a strange land," as aliens in a foreign country called Egypt. How they resemble the troubled and the poor among us!

Mary, too, becomes for us the connection to the Jewish roots of our faith tradition. Mary is the symbol of the people of Israel. She is the flower of the nation who, in the fullness of time, brought forth the fruit of her womb, Jesus. In the Hebrew Scriptures Israel is espoused to Yahweh their God. Mary gives birth to Jesus, the Son of God, and the Son of Israel. The ancient Hebrew motif in the stories of the miraculous nature of the conception and birth of such Biblical heroes as Isaac, Samson, and Samuel

THE WORD MADE ALIVE - THE PASTORAL WRITINGS OF

is perfected in the familiar nativity story of Jesus

The image of Mary does not stop with these infancy narratives of the gospels. For we see in Mary an image of true discipleship – the story of our own growth in faith, often overcoming discouragement and anxiety. Like modern mothers, Mary is the mother who loves her son, despite her inability at times to understand him. In Luke's gospel she searches for the 12-year-old Jesus, after losing him during the family pilgrimage to the temple in Jerusalem. Jesus responds to her anxious search for him by saying, "Didn't you know that I had to be about my Father's business?" Not comprehending, she faithfully "pondered these things in her heart." This is the image of faith, even in the face of doubt.

Just as Israel is described by the Hebrew prophets as the Spouse of Yahweh so Jesus is described in the New Testament scriptures as the bridegroom to whom is betrothed the

Church, the Bride of Christ. Just as Israel is the heir of the promises and blessing given by Yahweh to their ancestors, Abraham and Sarah, when He said, "I will make you the father of many nations," and "In you will I bless all the nations of the earth," so Jesus, as the son of Israel, becomes the heir of the promises and blessing of Israel. The Church, too, becomes joint heirs with Israel in these same promises when Jesus declared to the Church, "Behold your mother." The Mother of Jesus is the Mother of the Church. The Church is the daughter of the nation of Israel. In Mary Israel becomes the mother of the Christian Church. In her Judaism gives birth to Christianity!

As we honor Mary our Mother so we must honor the

57

people of Israel. As we honor Israel so we honor Mary the mother of Jesus our Messiah. So we can see in all of this that there is no place for anti-Semitism in the Catholic Church. We are to love Israel even as we love our blessed mother, Mary. The destinies of both Israel and the Church are inextricably bound together to the end of time by the same Shekinah, who led the Children of Israel from the bondage of Egypt into the place of freedom, who is identified as the Holy Spirit, poured out within the hearts of Christians, leading us out from the slavery of injustice into the marvelous freedom of the children of God.

For Catholics, as for Orthodox Christians, Mary reflects the image of God. The Orthodox Church teaches that we are being divinized – transformed into the image of Christ (2 Corinthians 3:18). Mary is the icon of that transformation – fully divinized, fully transformed by the glory of God. This is the reason she is given such high honor. She is the perfection of the Christian – one so aligned with Christ that she shares in the light of the divinity of her son. This is the deepest meaning of what Catholics call her "Assumption," and what Orthodox Christians call her "Dormition" ("falling asleep"). As she passed from this earthly life, she was fully embraced into the life of God – a future which awaits us all.

In Christ we celebrate the image God's life poured into human existence. In Mary we celebrate a human life being taken up into the very life of the holy Trinity – the divinization destined for us all. The ancient Christian writers were so struck by this connection of Mary to Christ that they identified her with "the woman clothed with the sun," a phrase found in the Book of Revelation which refers to the Church. Mary stands for the Church – a people clothed with God's light. She is the first Christian – the first to receive the good news of Christ and to respond with trust. In giving birth to Jesus, she brought forth the story of the Church – all those who would follow her "yes" to the call of God.

Throughout the centuries, Mary has given hope to the oppressed and comfort to the sick. In the Western Hemisphere, Our Lady of Guadalupe became a tender image to the poor native peoples who were often exploited. Her dark features resembled theirs, and her robes were those of a pregnant Aztec princess about to bring new life into the world. This image of Guadalupe would become the banner of liberation for the people of Mexico – her shrine in Mexico City one of the most visited in the world.

Recently, Marian devotion has been scrutinized, and sometimes downplayed as sentimental – off-track from a supposedly more enlightened faith. Marian images were said to reduce the role of women in the Church, limiting them to domestic life and placing them under the will of men. However, this is not the biblical image of Mary. In Luke 1:46-55, we find the greatest song of liberation in the scriptures placed into the mouth of Mary, who receives the transforming news of Christ as a daughter of Israel, a people oppressed by others for so long:

My soul proclaims the greatness of God,

And my spirit rejoices in God my Savior;

Who has looked with favor on this lowly servant

From this day all generations will call me blessed:

You, O God, have done great things for me,

and holy is Your Name.

You have mercy on those who fear you

in every generation.

You have shown the strength of your arm,

and scattered the proud in their conceit.

You have cast down the mighty from their thrones

and have lifted up the lowly.

You have filled the hungry with good things,

and the rich you have sent away empty.

You have come to the help of your servant Israel,

for you have remembered your promise of mercy...

It is my hope that this letter will lead to a re-examination of Marian devotion within our Communion. Mary is not a threat to the leadership of women in the Church; she is a sign of perseverance through oppression. Mary held to her faith in the face of her son's death, and through the biblical period when the authorities persecuted the first Christians. Her presence with the disciples is noted in the Acts of the Apostles, when the Holy Spirit comes upon them in the feast we celebrate as Pentecost. For Mary, this fulfills the first coming of the Spirit upon her, at the announcement of her role as the mother of the Messiah.

Mary is called the Mother of God. Our Orthodox sisters and brothers put it in another way: Mary is Theotokos. In English this literally means, "The God-bearer." Such an image of bearing the divine Christ into the world again becomes an icon for our own identities. We spiritually bear Christ into the world every day through our lives – our actions and our words. But these lofty thoughts remain just thoughts unless Mary becomes more than a picture for candles and devotion in a corner of the church.

The best known devotion associated with Mary is the rosary. It is a simple prayer to follow, but leads to profound spiritual transformation. The rosary teaches the importance of silence, and concentration on the presence of God. The mysteries of the rosary are not just old stories from the Bible. They are images that reflect the various joys and sorrows of our own lives. The rosary is a commitment to prayer. Those with regular devotion to the rosary are transformed into people of wisdom and peace.

It is easy to find short instructional booklets on the rosary – the traditional recitation of the rosary, and the recitation of the rosary with scripture quotes. The point of these aids is to help us begin to pray. This is a central meaning of Mary's iconic presence for the Church: Mary is the image of the Christian at prayer. She prayerfully pondered the events of her life in the light of faith. She is led by the Spirit of God into times of joy (Luke 1), and sheltered by God's providence through dark times of danger (Matthew 2:16). In all these biblical scenes, Mary finally returns to silence – a place to encounter our deepest self, and to encounter God. Mary's life is a message of hope and courage, and most deeply a message of trust. Such trust is only discovered through prayer.

I encourage you to begin your own Marian devotion. Perhaps this might be a thoughtful daily recitation of the Magnificat, from the first chapter of Luke's Gospel; or you might be drawn to the rosary. Some pray before a picture of Our Lady of Guadalupe, or another image of Mary from around the world. Different styles of prayer fit our different personal experiences and cultures. Marian devotion inspires us to make our lives sacred by remembering God's presence and guidance through the day. This is the beauty of prayer.

I close by drawing your attention to the words of Mary at the wedding feast at Cana. She instructed the wine servers to "Do whatever he says," – to follow the instructions of Jesus. Ancient Christian writers found inspiration in these words from John 2:1-11, for these words are at the very heart of the Christian call. The lesson goes even further because, when the wine servers bring great jars of ordinary water to Jesus, they find the water transformed into the best wine.

We, too, are called by Mary to "Do whatever he says." We bring our ordinary lives to Christ, and find them transformed into extraordinary lives of compassion and peace. May you find the courage of faith that Mary found early in her life. May you imitate her hope, bringing the love of her son, Jesus, into your own life and into the life of the world around you.

"Holy Mary, Mother of God, pray for us, now and at the hour of our death. Amen."

+ Bishop Peter Elder Hickman

Chapter 8

Can We Talk?

Introduction

A few years ago my cousin, Gregory Elder, after nearly twenty years an Episcopal priest was re-ordained a Roman Catholic priest in the nearby Roman Catholic Diocese of San Bernadino, California. This was done with the specific approval of Pope Benedict XVI despite the fact that Father Gregory is a married man with a daughter. I have often wondered how it has been for him to be the only married priest in a culture where all his peers must remain celibate. We have yet to have that conversation. Nonetheless, it does bring to our attention that Pope Benedict was willing to receive the clergy of other churches if those individuals were having problems with the leadership of their respective denomination. I must admit that I have done something similar as I have received many Roman Catholic priests into the Ecumenical Catholic Communion precisely because they were married and were no longer welcome in the church that ordained them. It was this stated policy of the Vatican that caused me to think about the importance of dialogue and conversation and our failure to really talk to each other about our differences within the Body of Christ. So I ask the question: Can we talk?

A pastoral Reflection

As I reflect on the recent troubles of the Anglican Communion – and our brother, Pope Benedict's recent response of inviting Anglicans to break with their communion and join the Roman Catholic Church – we are once again compelled to face the reality that church division and competition have always been major factors in the history of Christianity. Recall Paul's dismay with the factionalism of the Corinthians, "Is Christ divided? While there is jealousy and rivalry among you, are you not acting according to the flesh and behaving in an ordinary human way?" This also exposes a deeper question of how one can be a Christian at odds with other Christians. The emphasis is on the "how."

So often, the push in discussions of religion is to make distinctions and to emphasize our differences. I recently experienced just the opposite, when I made a presentation on the Eucharist and the ancient church to the students and faculty of Fuller Theological Seminary, a leading Evangelical Seminary. I explained the meaning and structure of the ancient liturgy of the Church, the vestments, the furnishings, the vessels, and the scriptural nature of the prayers. Their faces revealed the enlightenment that occurred within their hearts and minds as they listened with great openness and eager receptivity. The impression that many in the audience may have once had of a Catholic Eucharist that was no more than rigid formalism and dead ritualism now gave way to an overwhelming impression of deep beauty and rich spirituality.

We followed this lecture with the celebration of the Eucharist, in which a profound and Spirit-filled experience of worship and unity was entered into by all. This was no longer a discussion or disagreement about theological concepts, but an ineffable encounter with the Divine Mystery beyond human ideas. No one can argue with such an encounter with authentic communion. It simply is! We know the encounter in the "within" of our hearts, in a place that transcends ideas and concepts. And, we know the encounter in the mystical community, the Body of Christ, alive in our presence. Such an experience with Christ is primal and life-changing.

I have often noticed that when there is disagreement among people, we tend to emphasize our differences, and ignore our commonalities. I am told that in conflict resolution, a facilitator will usually try to help the parties involved to do just the opposite – to recognize and affirm with each other their areas of agreement. Then, and only then, will those in conflict have a foundation of commonality on which to build mutual understanding, rather than continuing an endless battle over their differences.

A truly ecumenical approach to the differences between Christian Churches – or even between Christian individuals – is to start with what is shared in common. And, what we share in common far exceeds the differences between us. This is the beginning of dialogue. This is the beginning of a partaking of the fruit of communion. Too often we refuse to speak with those "on the other side." We want them to accept our theological positions and ideas before we talk to them. We find virtue in "standing fast" with our point of view. In the midst of such pain and opposition, we make no headway, experience more fracturing of the Body of Christ, and, worse, miss the presence of God's grace in our midst – something characterized always by patience, love and peace.

The great Russian icon painter, Andre Rublev, created an icon of the Holy Trinity that is based upon the visitation of the three angels to Abraham and Sarah – from the Book of

Genesis. What is striking about this icon is that it depicts three heavenly beings involved in a conversation. The image of the three in conversation is meant to symbolize the Holy Trinity in that the conversation is central to the symbolism. We call this conversation "proceeding," as in the traditional description that the Spirit "proceeds from the Father."

My dear friend, Father Ned Reidy, recently shared with me concerning this word, "conversation." "Literally from the Latin it means to „turn to the other and face the other".....from "versus" and "con".....not just speak to the other alone....but to turn your body and even your chair to the other as a sense of honoring the other...but also it is a silent declaration that at this moment you and your words are such a gift to me that I stop everything else in order to honor you...this moment and your words...to literally hang on every word and sound that comes forward from you to me...it's a wonderful image and again reflecting the communion and intimacy of the dialogue."

So conversation means life. All life is a conversation – a give and take between two or more who share a common life, a communion of being. Marriage is a conversation of body and soul. Even the Eucharist is a solemn conversation – an ebb and flow between the Body of Christ and the members of His Body each in their respective roles.

In its totality (proclamation of the word, sign of peace, Holy Eucharist, etc.) it is an experience of God, for it is an experience of connection, acceptance, and oneness. Again, it is a communion (koinonia) of being. Jesus prayed that this conversation might never end. In John 17:21, he asked that all might be one in the same way as He is one with the Father. His oneness with the Father is unity in diversity –

the unity not eliminating the distinction, but maintaining it through the oneness of love. Again, this is communion of love. Without love is there is no communion.

The great task of the Ecumenical Catholic Communion is the prophetic call for a conversation both within, among ourselves, and without, among those who are not affiliated with our particular ecclesial structure. (This, by the way, is why we participate, in a supportive way, with our sisters and brothers in the Roman Catholic Reform Movement as well as with our sisters and brothers in the Anglican Communion.) Though our own ECC communities vary in style, we are in conversation – hoping to find parallels before we point out the differences. Our ideas might differ, our limited understanding of the infinite and unknowable mystery might differ, but the call of the Spirit is for us to maintain a communion that will affirm our basic Catholic identity.

So we actively seek to engage others – in the Roman Catholic Church, the Anglican Communion, the Old Catholic Union of Utrecht, other Catholic and Apostolic Churches, Evangelical Churches and those Churches further from the Catholic tradition. Competition is not the call of the Gospel. It never was. Conversation is the call – conversation so deep that it quickly turns into a divine encounter – the Spirit speaking from heart to heart, taking us from glory to glory. This, by definition, is authentic communion, koinonia!

The lecture at Fuller began as a conversation, and was completed as an experience of authentic communion. It so bonded all those present, that no one walked away doubting God's presence among us. This is the hallmark of true ecumenism. This is the great work of the Ecumenical

Catholic Communion. We are to call those who have been left outside such a conversation into a dialogue that will result in a realization of a holy communion of Love.

We began by calling those marginalized by the Church: divorced people, married priests, gay and lesbian people, women seeking ordination, those damaged by a painful experience of a divided church. Now we must also turn back and engage with those who seemed to be the ones marginalizing people. Too often we have characterized them as "the enemy." Jesus cautions us about this. Christians are to have no enemies, for they are to love their perceived enemies and pray for those who persecute them.

The wonderful Christian saint and writer, Corrie ten Boom, was a prisoner in a Nazi concentration camp, and saw her sister die there. She was eventually released from the concentration camp. After the war, she first founded a place of recovery for the victims of such Nazi camps – that they might be healed in body and heart. But, the next place she founded was for the former guards in the Nazi camps. She realized that they too were victims. Their hearts were so damaged that they were able to inflict tremendous pain on other human beings. They would suffer from the memories of their own cruelty.

Though we do not often deal with such extreme circumstances, we find conflict and anger in the very human hearts of the Church. The Ecumenical Catholic Communion – every member – is called to this ministry of reconciliation. It is not enough to protest the injustice of the past. We must actively seek to heal such brokenness caused by religious injustice and intolerance. If we do not, the infection of anger remains, and the pain manifests itself in harsh meetings, troubling encounters with each other, emotional bruises that will not heal, and resentment that leads to a broken communion. We cannot afford such pain at the cost of hope and peace. And,

more importantly, the larger Body of Christ cannot afford such pain and division at the cost of hope and peace.

What we can afford is time – time for conversation and for relationship. If we reflect this quality of the Holy Trinity within our communion, within our local communities, and within our personal relationships, we shall discover the beauty and power of the Three-in-One in our very hearts which is a sharing in the very life of God.

Chapter 9

Discerning the Word of God
(The Word of the Lord)

Introduction

Having been raised in an Evangelical Protestant home of the Baptist kind. My mother was a deaconess and Sunday School teacher as my father was a deacon and Sunday School teacher. The earliest stories that were read to me as a young child were the stories of the Bible. I grew to love the Scriptures and many of its passages and verses I had committed to memory. I had memorized the list of the canonical books of the Bible in their proper order and I learned to quote chapter and verse as any good Evangelical Christian would. For me like most Evangelicals the Bible was the Word of God. As such, we placed a great burden on the biblical writers by imposing on them the status of inerrancy. I came to realize in my own theological development that this was an overly simplistic view of Sacred Scripture and often led to crudely literal interpretations of the texts and using the verses of the biblical writings as proof texts of an assumed theological supposition. This often leads to an abuse of the Scriptures in pastoral work and an inevitable legalistic religion. In this chapter I struggle toward an understanding of the Word of God which is the revelatory experience to which Scripture points. I ask what is the relationship between the Word of God and the written texts of the biblical writers. This is my attempt toward a theology of Scripture that would lead to a better method of interpretation for these ancient texts.

The Word of the Lord

The Hebrew use of the phrase, "The Word of the Lord" (אֵלַי בַּר־יְהוָהד) nearly always refers to a dynamic and direct encounter of a human person or persons with the Divine self communication or expression which is initiated by the Divine person. The Divine Word is an intentional expression of the Divine life that is identified with the Divine Life. (i.e. the Word was God John 1:1, 8). In the New Testament the Word is identified as the second person of the Blessed Trinity that became incarnate in the historical person of Jesus Christ. Jesus is the ultimate expression, the final Word, of the Divine Life (Hebrews 1:1). The Divine Word originates in the Divine person of the Father (Abba) who generates the Divine person of the Word, the eternally begotten Son. The Word of the Lord is God the eternal Son who became incarnate through the power (dynamic) of the Holy Spirit by the will (intention) of the Father.

In the Hebrew Bible the Word of the Lord is always identified with the Divine person and never to a written text. The Scripture bears witness to the Word but in and of itself is not the Word. The various scriptures that make up both the Hebrew Bible and the Christian New Testament are, for us, a primary witness, after that of the eye witness recipients of the Word. "What was from the beginning, what we have heard, what we have seen with our eyes, what we have looked at and touched with our hands, concerning the Word of Life; and the life was manifested, and we have seen and testify and proclaim to you the eternal life, which was with the Father and was manifested to us. What we have seen and heard we proclaim to you also, so that you too may have fellowship with us; and indeed our fellowship is with the Father, and with His Son Jesus Christ. These things we write, so that our joy may be made complete (1 John 1:1-4) Jesus makes this point to the Pharisees when He said, "You search the Scriptures, thinking that in them you have eternal life, not realizing that the Scripture bear witness of Me." (John 5:39). The Holy Spirit is the primary witness par excellence of the Divine Word.

"But the Paraclete, the Holy Spirit, whom the Father will send in My name, will teach you all things" (John 14:26).

As Catholic Christians we also affirm that the Apostolic Tradition, both written and oral, as the Apostle Paul writes, "...stand firm and hold to the traditions which you were taught, whether by word of mouth or by written letter from us" (2 Thess. 2:15) is also a primary witness to the Divine Word. This witness is to be found in the ongoing life of the Church and finds its best expression in the Divine Liturgy (Worship, Latira) of the baptized, the People of God. We also affirm that reason is another witness to the Word of God, "'Come, let us reason together' says the LORD" (Isaiah 1:8). Human experience through the realm of the senses and interaction with the world is yet another witness to the Word, "Ever since the creation of the world, His invisible attributes of eternal power and divinity have been able to be understood and perceived in what He has made" (Romans 1:20). Finally, holy men and women, the saints of all the ages bear witness to the Word of God (i.e. John the Baptist, see John 5:32-35) within the inner workings of the human soul. The inner religious inclination of the soul seems to be intrinsic to our humanity as the universality of the phenomena of religion in all human cultures seems to suggest. The Hebrew and Christian

Scriptures may be one of the most important witnesses to the Word but it is one among many. Sola Scriptura is insufficient and does not take into account the great cloud of witnesses to the Word.

The Idolatry of Biblicism

To worship is to ascribe the highest place to the object worshipped. Whatever one makes as their ultimate value, concern, standard for life is one's god. If that object is anything other than the Divine Creator then that object is a false God. Idolatry is to worship, to make one's highest value, a creature in place of the Creator (Romans 1:23). Biblicism is an idolatry of a creature, the written text of the biblical writings. (This was the great weakness of the Pharisees. Biblicism can be compared to the practice of Islam as an extreme example in their idolatry of the written text called the Koran). In the hands of the Biblicist the text of scripture becomes static and the dynamic nature of the Word of God as an interaction between humanity and the Divine life all but disappears. The Word of God is realized and recognized only in the dynamic interaction between the Divine and the human. In the absence of that dynamic the Scripture is robbed of its power to bear witness for it is the Spirit that gives life while the letter kills (2Cor. 3:6).

Nowhere in the Scriptures is the Word of God identified with the text. The Word of God is something other to which the text bears witness. Nowhere in the texts of the Bible is there a claim that everything that is written therein is inspired. Nowhere in the texts of the Bible is a cannon provided for determining the inspiration of a given book. Nowhere in the Biblical texts is there a claim of inerrancy and infallibility. The inerrancy of Scripture is an external philosophical concept that is imposed upon the biblical writings in order to provide support for the authority of an absolute certainty needed for the domination of a particular theological point of view to be imposed over that of others apart from the dynamic of dialogue that is so very necessary in the process of discerning the Word of God.

Discerning the Word of God

Discovering the Word of God in a written text necessarily involves discernment. This discernment is achieved through interacting with the written texts. We must engage the biblical writers in dialogue in order to discover the Word of God hidden within the text. This requires the use of all the sources of revelation: the Canonical Scriptures; Tradition of the people of God; Reason; and human experience (especially science). John Wesley's quad-lateral comes to mind here: Scripture, Tradition, Reason, and Experience.

The Four Levels of the Way of Discernment:

1) The Way of Instruction (Torah) Law.

2) The Way of Justice (the Prophets).

3) The Way of Wisdom (the Writings).

4) The Way of Love (Jesus) Gospel.

The Way of love begins with the Divine initiative (Incarnation). The surrender of the "self" must follow in the response of the human soul. Then comes the baptism of the Holy Spirit.

A Case Study: How the early church engaged the

Scriptures and changed a fundamental command of Scripture and Tradition in receiving the Gentiles into the church without requiring circumcision:

The Two Kinds of Laws within the Torah

In looking at all the instructions (commandments, statutes, and ordinances) recorded in the Scriptures (both the Hebrew Bible and the Christian New Testament) it is necessary to distinguish between codes of essentially two different kinds (see Thomas Aquinas):

1) **Justice Codes** (those laws that correspond with the Natural Law) are that which have to do with fairness and equity. (Iniquity: the opposite of equity). The Golden Rule of Jesus "Do unto others what you would have them do unto you" as well as the Confucian Principle of Jen, "Do not do to others what you would not like them to do to you" which is the fundamental virtue of the Confucian teaching of goodness and benevolence. It is expressed through recognition of value and concern for others, no matter their rank or class. This rule summarizes the Natural Law that forms the basis of all justice codes including those found in the Torah. This would include all laws that forbid the violation of the rights and dignity of another person. It is unjust to exploit another; to deprive another of their life (You shall not murder), their family (You shall not commit adultery), their land or means of economic survival (You shall not covet), their proper possessions (You shall not steal); their reputation (You shall not bear false witness against thy neighbor); their dignity (You shall honor thy father and mother).

Justice Codes reflect the universal, absolute, and unchanging values of the Divine Life. To love God and neighbor is always valid and binding upon the individual person and the human community in all times and in all places. Justice codes reflect that which is constant in what is recognized as the good, the true, and the beautiful in human relations. It has always been a violation of justice to commit murder (the taking of an innocent life) for whatever reason and it will always be as long as humanity exists. (This is why the death penalty is ultimately unjust because we cannot be absolutely certain of one's guilt).

Some of the prescriptions of the Torah regulating human sexual behavior are, in fact, justice codes. Sexual promiscuity remains unjust because it necessarily involves the exploitation of others. It does this by objectifying and depersonalizing the other as a mere instrument or means to self gratification apart from love of that other. It is behavior that violates the human dignity (Imago Dei) of a person or persons; it is an activity directed toward human persons that does violence to the Imago Dei that is intrinsic to every human person and thus becomes an act against God whose image we are.

2) **Holiness Codes** (those laws and taboos that have no necessary connection with issues of justice and/or morality. Holiness has to do with the setting apart (Sanctification or consecration) of a person (a people), place, or thing, or any other created thing for the exclusive use and unique possession of a divine being. Holiness codes give outward sign or expression to the identity of any of the above as being the exclusive possession of the Divine life. The laws concerning circumcision, the Sabbath, attire, and other such visible expression are essentially cultic in nature and are designed to preserve the identity of any of the above with the Divine Life to which it has

been dedicated.

Holiness codes are relative to the circumstances and purposes for which they were established and are subject to change as the circumstances demand and according to the divine economy. Justice codes always take precedence over holiness codes. Jesus taught that if a holiness code in its application violates a justice code then it is the justice code that takes precedence. In the New Testament no justice code of the Hebrew Scriptures is ever discarded. However, we have numerous examples of holiness codes being rejected, changed, or discarded. Jesus Himself demonstrated this in His frequent violation of a holiness code, of keeping Sabbath, when confronted with a justice issue such as the obligation to meet human need or to alleviate suffering. He healed on the Sabbath, harvested food on the Sabbath, instructed others to work by carrying objects on the Sabbath. He also violated the holiness codes regarding ablutions (ceremonial washings).

The Gentile Question

The first major controversy in the Church occurred in the first generation: the question of whether or not Gentiles could be admitted into the Christian community without observing Torah and specifically the requirement of circumcision.

The Party of James and the Jerusalem Church: The followers of James the brother of Jesus and the leader of the mother church in Jerusalem, who were the conservatives and are often referred to as the Judaizers, took the position that all gentiles were required to observe Torah as part of their initiation into the Church. They had the weight of the witness of both the Scriptures and

Tradition on their side, and could even quote Jesus as saying, "Do not think that I came to abolish the Law or the Prophets; I did not come to abolish but to fulfill. For truly I say to you, until heaven and earth pass away, not the smallest letter or stroke shall pass from the Law until all is accomplished. Whoever then annuls one of the least of these commandments, and teaches others to do the same, shall be called least in the kingdom of heaven; but whoever keeps and teaches them, he shall be called great in the kingdom of heaven." (Matthew 5:17-19)

The Party of Peter and Paul and the Antioch Church: Peter, Paul, and Barnabas, on the other hand., who were of the great missionary church at Antioch took the position that the Gentile converts need not observe Torah but merely had to be baptized in the name of the Lord Jesus to be received into the Christian community. They had the weight of experience and reason on their side. How did they resolve this conflict?

The First Ecumenical Council (Synod): They did so by discerning the Word of God (the mind of the Holy Spirit) in the matter through the practice of prayerful dialogue at the first Ecumenical Council of the Church held in Jerusalem. It was while they were in council that they discerned the witness of the Spirit, the Paraclete, concerning the Word of the Lord. It was in Council through a process of discernment in a dynamic prayerful dialogue that the Word of God was discovered that brought an end to the conflict so that the Apostles and Presbyters could confidently and unanimously claim, "it seemed good to the Holy Spirit and to us..."

These followers of Jesus of the first generation Church in their rejection of the practice of circumcision in the admission and initiation of Gentile believers into the Christian community; in their dropping of the requirement of Sabbath observance and the observance of other festivals mandated by Moses; and the modification of dietary laws (Acts 15:19-20) did so while in council. This sets a precedent for the Church that the believing community when meeting in an Ecumenical Council has the authority to bind and loose as the Holy Spirit leads all holiness laws. Authority to discern the Word has been given by Christ (Who is the Word) to the Church by means of the witness of the Holy Spirit of Truth who leads into all truth.

This controversy teaches us something very important about the source of authority in the Church and how it is to be exercised. First, it must be recognized that Christ is the only One who possesses all authority and who has the freedom to delegate that authority to whomever He pleases by virtue of His passion. "All authority has been given to Me in heaven and earth" (Matthew 28:18). Christ, who is the only head of the Church by virtue of the fact that He has purchased and consecrated her by His own blood, delegates this authority to the Church as recorded in the Gospel of Matthew:

"I will give you the keys of the kingdom of heaven; and whatever you bind (forbid) on earth shall have been bound (forbidden) in heaven, and whatever you loose (permit) on earth shall have been loosed (permitted) in heaven." (Matthew 16-19) "Truly I say to you, whatever you bind (forbid) on earth shall have been bound (forbidden) in heaven; and whatever you loose (permit) on earth shall have been loosed (permitted) in heaven. (Matthew 18-18)

In the rabbinic tradition these words would have been

understood as God delegating to the believing community the authority to resolve questions of custom and practice.

The Homosexual Question

As the Gentile question was to the first generation church so the question concerning homosexual persons is for our generation. Are the prohibitions of the Hebrew Scriptures and the New Testament writings against homosexuality and homosexual relationships justice codes that corresponds to natural law and therefore not subject to change or are these prohibitions to be classified as holiness codes that are subject to change by the community's God-granted authority to bind and to loose as the Spirit directs. Granted that the holiness codes of the Book of Leviticus forbids homosexual acts and as a consequence the culture of first century Judaism strongly rejected and condemned all homosexual behavior and persons. And granted that the Apostle Paul clearly seems to share with his Jewish cultural heritage this rejection and condemnation of homosexual behavior and persons. Do we, as the Church, have the authority to discern the Word of God in the midst of this question? Does the Church have the authority to question the writings of Paul in order to determine what portions are indeed inspired and what portions are not? Does the experience of the Apostle Peter in regard to the Gentile question teach us anything that can help us with the homosexual question in our time! Can we, in regard to this question like Peter and the Gentile question come to realize "that I should not designate any man unholy and unclean?" (Acts 10:28)

Should not we, as the Church, discern this question in prayerful dialogue using all the witnesses of the Word of God at our disposal? Can the dynamic interchange between the witness of the Bible, Tradition, reason, and experience enable us to discover the Word of the Lord in this matter so that we can say as was said before by our ancestors, "It seems good to the Holy Spirit and to us"?

Final Note on the Doctrine of the Inspiration of Scripture

Two texts on which the claim of an inerrant text rests:

2 Timothy 3:16

πασα γραφη Θεοπνευστος και ωφελιμος προς διδασκαλιαν προς ελεγμον προς

pasa graphe Theopneustos kai ophelimos pros didaskalian pros elegmon pros

Every scripture God-breathed and profitable for teaching for reproof for

επανορθωσιν προς παιδειαν την εν δικαιοσυνη

epanorthosin pros paidayan tane in dikaisunay.

Correction for training the in righteousness.

All Divinely inspired (God-breathed) writings remain profitable for teaching, for reproof, for correction, for training in righteousness; so that the person of God may be adequate, equipped for every good work. (Translation mine)

American Standard Version: Every scripture inspired of God is also profitable for teaching, for reproof, for correction, for instruction which is in righteousness.

The Greek word "graphe" simply means "writing." It is a

generic word designating any written text. To say "all scripture" would be the same as saying "all writings." The English words writings and scripture have synonymous meaning. That is they are identical in meaning and therefore interchangeable. The use by the author of the phrase, "all scripture" or "all writings" is not intended to say that any and all written texts are inspired (God breathed). To then claim that the writer is saying that all canonical writings are inspired cannot be supported by this text. For he is writing this statement before there ever was a canon of inspired writings. What is actually being written is better rendered as "All Divinely inspired writings... ".

The writer does not use the verb "to be" (is) in this phrase. Moreover, The writer gives no indication of which writings are considered inspired in his mind and which are not. From this verse we come to know only one thing: that there are some writings that are God breathed and by implication there are some writings which are not. The question remains: What writings are indeed inspired and what are not. This not the same as asking what writings are canonical and what are not. Then follows the next two questions: 1) Are there inspired writings not included in the Jewish or Christian canons? And 2) are all canonical writings inspired? Could a given biblical document have portions that are inspired and other portions that are not. In practice this seems to be a common approach even among those who claim that all biblical texts are inerrant.

2 Peter 1: 20-21

τουτο πρωτον γινωσκοντες οτι πασα προφητεια γραφης ιδιας επιλυσεως ου γινεται ου γαρ θεληματι ανθρωπου ηνεχθη προφητεια ποτε αλλα υπο πνευματος αγιου φερομενοι ελαλησαν απο Θεου ανθρωποι

But know this first of all, that no prophecy of Scripture is a matter of one's own interpretation, for no prophecy was ever made by an act of human will, but men moved by the Holy Spirit spoke from God.

Again, the author is saying that by definition all written prophecy comes from those moved of the Holy Spirit and spoke from God. Prophecy by definition is inspired communication by means of the Holy Spirit. The question remains: Are all the biblical (canonical) writings and texts, indeed any and all written words, in the Bible prophetic?

The Word as Person

Genesis 15-1: After these things the Word of the LORD came to Abram in a vision, saying (speaking),

"Do not fear, Abram, I am a shield to you; Your very great reward."

Genesis 15-4: Then behold, the Word of the LORD came to him, saying (speaking), "This man will not be your heir; but one who will come forth from your own body, he shall be your heir."

Exodus 9-20: The one among the servants of Pharaoh who feared the Word of the LORD made his servants and his livestock flee into the houses;

Exodus 9-21: but he who paid no regard to the Word of the LORD left his servants and his livestock in the field.

Numbers 3-16: So Moses counted them, as he was

commanded by the Word of the LORD.

In the above mentioned texts from the Torah, the phrase, "the Word of the Lord" does not refer to a written text but to a self expression of a divine person identified as Yahweh.

The Word of the Lord in Ezekiel the Prophet:

6:1 "Thus the Word of the Lord came to me..."

7:1 "Thus the Word of the Lord came to me..."

11:14 "Thus the Word of the Lord came to me..."

12:1 "Thus the Word of the Lord came to me..."

12:8 "Thus the Word of the Lord came to me..."

12:21 "Thus the Word of the Lord came to me..."

13:1 "Thus the Word of the Lord came to me..."

14:2 "the Word of the Lord came to me..."

14:12 "Thus the Word of the Lord came to me..."

15:1 "Thus the Word of the Lord came to me..."

16:1 "Thus the Word of the Lord came to me..."

17:1 "Thus the Word of the Lord came to me..."

17:11 "Thus the Word of the Lord came to me..."

18:1 "Thus the Word of the Lord came to me..."

20:2 "Then the Word of the Lord came to me..."

21:21 "Thus the Word of the Lord came to me..."

21:13 "Thus the Word of the Lord came to me…"

21:23 "Thus the Word of the Lord came to me…"

22:1 "Thus the Word of the Lord came to me…"

22: 17 "Thus the Word of the Lord came to me…"

23:1 "Thus the Word of the Lord came to me…"

24:1 "On the tenth day of the tenth month, in the ninth year, the Word of the Lord came to me…"

24:15 "Thus the Word of the Lord came to me…"

25:1 "Thus the Word of the Lord came to me…"

26:1 "On the first day of the …….. month in the eleventh year, the Word of the Lord came to me…"

27:1 "Thus the Word of the Lord came to me…"

28:1 "Thus the Word of the Lord came to me…"

28:20 "Thus the Word of the Lord came to me…"

29:1 "On the twelfth day of the tenth month in the tenth year the Word of the Lord came to me…"

29:17 "On the first day of the first month in the twenty-seventh year, the Word of the Lord came to me…"

30:1 "Thus the Word of the Lord came to me…"

30:20 "On the seventh day of the first month in the eleventh year the Word of the Lord came to me…"

31:1 "On the first day of the third month in the eleventh year the Word of the Lord came to me…"

32:1 "On the first day of the twelfth month in the twelfth year, the Word of the Lord came to me…"

32:17 "On the fifteenth day of the first month in the twelfth year, the Word of the Lord came to me…"

33:1 "Thus the Word of the Lord came to me…"

33:23 "Thus the Word of the Lord came to me…"

34:1 "Thus the Word of the Lord came to me…"

35:1 "Thus the Word of the Lord came to me…"

36:1-2 "…hear the Word of the Lord! (Yahweh) Thus says the Lord God…(Adoni Elohim)

36:16 "Thus the Word of the Lord came to me…"

37:15 "Thus the Word of the Lord came to me…"

38:1 "Thus the Word of the Lord came to me…"

In each case the writer, Ezekiel the prophet, in his use of the expression, "the Word of the Lord" designates a divine person not a written text. His hearers would understand that as well. When the prophet is using this expression, the hearers would not be thinking of the text of Torah or the texts of any canonical writings of the other prophets, they would be thinking of a divine person speaking through a dynamic personal encounter with the prophet. In this case the Divine Word is a person engaging a human person. This is experiential and subjective for the prophet Ezekiel.

The Question of Authority

Where is divine authority to be found?

Jesus Christ possesses all authority in Heaven and on earth. (Matthew 28:18)This authority belongs only to Him. It is His exclusive possession by virtue of the fact that He, and He alone, is the Word of the Lord made flesh.

He delegates His authority to the Church (John 20:20). Witnesses to this authority of Jesus in the Church are the four: Scripture, Tradition, Reason, and Experience. The Holy Spirit works through these for witnesses in order to enable the followers of Christ to discern the Word of God, a living dynamic person who is none other than Jesus Christ.

Scripture is not the incarnation of the Divine Word. Jesus is the only incarnation of the eternal Word of God. Christ becomes incarnationally present to the Church in a derived sense through the Sacraments and the He who is the Word of God becomes present to us through the Four Witnesses when they are in dialogue with each other. This dialogue is best expressed in the context of the Ecumenical Council (see Acts 15). Therefore the ultimate authority of Christ is most clearly expressed in the context of the Ecumenical Council.

Examples of Texts of the Scriptures that Are Not Inspired

The Census of David (see 2 Samuel 24 and compare with 1 Chronicles 21)

Jude's citation of Enoch (Jude 14)

Paul's remark, "O stupid Galatians!" Compare with what Jesus said in the Sermon on the Mount, "But I say to you, whoever is angry with his brother will be liable to judgment, and whoever says to his brother 'Raqa' (stupid, imbecile, idiot) will be answerable to the Sanhedrin, and whoever says 'You fool' will be liable to the fires of Gehenna."

The texts of Scripture often contain inspired statements that are of the Word of God. But the texts of Scripture often contain statements which are not inspired, not the Word of God. We need to "rightly divide" the Word from the text itself. This is what discernment means. It requires study and dioloque with all the witnesses of revelation and truth.

Questions That We Must Ask

What is the nature of Scripture?

Are the various writings that make up the canonical scriptures (i.e. the Bible) the Word of God or are they collectively the vehicle by which the Word of God is communicated to us?

Can we make a distinction between the Word of God and the vehicle (the scripture) which conveys the Word of God?

The Word of God by definition must be inerrant. Does the vehicle (the written text) itself need to be inerrant in order to be adequate to the job of conveying the Word of God to us?

Is the adequacy of the Bible to convey the Word of God dependent on an inerrancy of the written text?

It is to these questions that we pursue as we seek to understand the mystery of God's self revelation to humanity through our study of the Bible.

Chapter 10

Reflections for Special Days

Introduction

I now conclude this book by sharing some thoughts regarding those important events in the life and work of Jesus that we, as Catholics, celebrate on special days in the Church year. Each year we follow a liturgical calendar so that as we commemorate the saving event of the life, death, and resurrection of Jesus we never lose sight of the narrative of Salvation Story in Jesus Christ. The respective stories of our own individual lives only have meaning when they are connected to the big story of the mystery of God's creating and saving action unfolding in human history.

The Mystery of Christmas is the Incarnation of God n Christ

Saint Athanasius of Alexandria wrote in the fourth century concerning the mystery of the Incarnation that "God became human in order that humanity might become divine." As we approach the celebration of yet another Christmas we are again reminded of one of the central mysteries of the Christian Faith, the mystery of God's appearance in human flesh for indeed that is the literal meaning of the Latin expression, "incarnation" or, rather, the "en-fleshment" of God.

In the person of Jesus of Nazareth God becomes for us a human being. As it is written by the first century writer of the Letter to the Hebrews, "He was made like us in all things save sin." This early Christian belief is not something that was made up by later generations of Christians or an idea that gradually evolved over the passing decades following the first century, but was something at the very heart of the Christian witness from the very beginning. "Beloved, I am not writing you an innovative instruction but the same instruction that you have had from the very beginning (I John 3:7 translation mine).

In the earliest written material of the New Testament documents, material written less than twenty years after the death and resurrection of Jesus, we encounter this startling belief. Startling because it was a belief embraced by Jews whose transcendent monotheism would have made it very improbable for them to be inclined to invent such a notion as God becoming a living and breathing human being just like one of us. Yet this is precisely what we find coming from the testimony proclaimed (kerygma) by the friends and eyewitnesses of Jesus.

And just what exactly were they saying? Paul, a learned rabbi, quoting a very early hymn from the Christian liturgy, wrote that Jesus the Messiah "is the image (Greek: εικων, icon) of the invisible God; that in Jesus "all the divine fullness was pleased to dwell" (Colossians 1: 15, 19). And in another hymn that Paul quotes, "though Jesus was in the very form of God, he did not regard equality with God as something to be exploited, but emptied himself, taking the form of a servant, coming in human likeness, and found in human appearance" (Philippians 2). Likewise, the writer to the Hebrews asserts that Jesus is "the radiance of God's glory, the very imprint of God's being" in human flesh. But it is in the Gospel of John that we find the classic expression that the eternal Word, who is God, "became flesh and dwelt among us. We beheld his glory, the splendor of the unique one of God."

This, then, is what we are celebrating and bearing witness to at Christmas. But this is only a part of the mystery that we celebrate. Remember what Saint Athanasius said at the beginning of this reflection? "God became human in order that humanity might become divine." Herein is the meaning of the divine action of God in the incarnation. It is nothing less than the full identification of human life with that of the divine life.

This is the whole point. This is the Divine purpose behind this incredible mystery of incarnation. In the person of Jesus God partook of our humanity with all our frailty and limitations, even the dreaded limitation of mortality. In the person of Jesus humanity becomes a partaker of the divine nature with all its endless wonder and unlimited potentiality, even the potentiality of endless life.

What we are presently, are earthen vessels holding a hidden treasure of divine life ready to be given birth. As the Apostle wrote, "what we shall be has not yet been revealed. But we do know that when Christ appears we shall be like Him, and we shall see Him just as He is." And as Paul says, "At present we see dimly as through a clouded glass, but then we shall see face to face. At present we know only partially; then we shall know fully, even as we are fully known." This, my brothers and sisters, is the mystery that we are about to celebrate this Christmas.

This is the essence of the mystery of Holy Christmas: In the birth of Jesus divinity becomes human and in our new birth in Christ we, in our common humanity, become Divine! This is not only the mystery we celebrate in the

Feast of Christmas; it is the mystery that we live out each day of our lives. May the Life of Christ be manifest in you not only at every Christmas but always!

The Holy Season of Lent

This ancient Christian observance is the forty day period of time preceding Easter in which the People of God prepare for the celebration of the Paschal Mystery of Christ, His suffering, death, and resurrection, in the Liturgy of the Triduum during Holy Week. In this great mystery Christ offers Himself for the life of the World.

We are now invited to walk with Christ in the Lenten journey. The Gospels remind us that Jesus set his face toward the Holy City of Jerusalem to make the final journey of this life, a journey to His appointed encounter with death. In Lent We are invited to participate in this same journey of Christ. It is a journey of the Spirit. It is a journey that is not without it's own peculiar kind of suffering. It is a journey that culminates in that fateful encounter with the mystery of death.

Is death then, the final destination of our life's journey? It may seem to us that death is our final destiny but our faith in Jesus tells us otherwise. The Paschal Mystery of Christ tells us that there is something beyond the horizon of death. It is a new kind of life, a transformed life, an eternally abundant life with unending possibility. This is so because it is the divine life, the life that is in Christ. This superior kind of life has now become our life that is hidden in God in Christ. Lent reminds us that we are in Christ.

So now we carry within us, through God's grace, the dying of Jesus so that we may share in the rising of Jesus to that ever new and glorified life which is impossible for death to overcome. During the journey of Lent we are invited to embrace death, to wrestle with the angel of death in the desert of our lives. It is the death of our "self-life", the death of the egocentric life which ever seems to be our natural inclination. As we die to our selfishness, our self interests, our "rights" we experience the power of the dying of Jesus within us so that the abundant life of Jesus may also become manifest in us.

This is not only true in the future day of our resurrection but it must be true even now in our present life. It is a realized eschatology. It is in the here and now of our lives that we are called to realize the manifestation of the uncreated light of Christ's life. Like the experience of Mount Tabor we are to be transfigured so that the light of Christ illuminates our world of the here and now, the extraordinary in the midst of the ordinary, the divine in the midst of that which is the essence of our humanity.

Therefore let us bear holy fruit as the evidence that we are with Christ on His journey to that great rendezvous with destiny, of the cross and the ultimate victory of the resurrection. Let us bear the fruit, in this Lenten Season, of love, joy, peace, patience, and self control. This is the fruit of the Holy Spirit. It is the fruit that bears the seed of this eternal life found in Jesus the Christ.

We cultivate this fruit of the Spirit in our deliberate and mindful observance of the Three Lenten Practices: prayer (both in personal devotion and in the communal celebration of the Liturgy), giving to the poor (the sharing of our gifts with others who cannot repay in kind), and fasting and abstinence (a practice that strengthens the life of Christ within us).

We begin this Lenten journey, on the day called Ash Wednesday, with the distribution of ashes marked as a cross upon our foreheads with the words "Remember that you are dust and to dust you shall return." This reminds us of our mortality, it reminds us of the death of Christ. It also reminds us of that blessed hope of our share in the resurrection of Christ to a new and glorified life. May God bless you as we journey together with Christ and one another into the deeper life of God!

The Journey of Lent, a Journey with Christ

In our Lenten observance we continue together on our collective journey with Jesus Christ toward Holy Week and our encounter with the Great Pascal Mystery of His suffering, death, and resurrection.

It is never too late to join in on the parade and now is as good as time as any to come along with the rest of your companions in faith as we make our way to the Holy City! We have already journeyed through the desert of testing with Christ as He, in his own humanity, confronted the power of the spirit of evil. We have climbed the Mount of Transfiguration and beheld the uncreated light of Christ's divinity, and were overcome by the cloud of the Holy Spirit, and heard the voice of the Father; an encounter with the mystery of the Divine Trinity. Now we will go with Jesus to Jerusalem to confront the corruption of religious institutionalism as He cleanses the Holy Temple in righteous indignation.

The first Sunday in Lent we had been reminded that we all must engage the reality of evil within the depths of our own hearts. The second Sunday in Lent we had been reminded of the great hope of our future Transformation and that of all creation in the Transfiguration of Christ. In the Third Sunday of Lent we will be reminded of our constant call to struggle against the systemic evils of our social institutions including our religious institutions in the world.

In this journey of the Spirit we are called to clear our eyes and see things as they really are and to see ourselves as we really are. We do this so that like Jesus we will be able to see things as they can be and ourselves as what we can become through our participation in Christ's Paschal Mystery.

So let us continue our journey in our active involvement in prayer, both personal and communal; in works of charity; and in the discipline of abstinence; that we may prove ourselves to be faithful co-workers with Christ for the salvation of all the world.

The Message of Lent: "You Must Be Born Again."

Under the cover of the darkness of night Nicodemus, a Pharisee and a distinguished rabbinical scholar of Torah, secretly sought an audience with Jesus while in the ancient holy city of Jerusalem.

The Gospel According to John records this clandestine conversation between the two rabbis and what unfolds is some of the most startling words ever spoken by Jesus. So staggering were the things that were said by Jesus that Nicodemus was incredulous yet at the same time he was strangely drawn to what seemed to be a new revelation of the coming Kingdom of God in the person of this obscure teacher from Galilee. It was during this exchange that Jesus utters the words of one of the best known and most often quoted verses of the entire Christian Bible, "For God so loved the world that He gave His only begotten Son, so that whoever believes in Him should not perish but have eternal life." Within these words of Jesus, Christians throughout the centuries have recognized the heart of the Gospel of Christ.

In these words we are told that the ultimate being, God, who is the source of all reality, all forms and all particular things, is also the source of the highest and noblest dynamic in all existence, the power of love.

Love has its ultimate beginning in the hidden mystery of the Divine Life. What we glimpse of God in these words is that the Son is begotten within this hidden Life of God. We are also shown that the Son is the Beloved of God, the God who created the world and proclaimed it good; the God who formed humanity from the dust of the earth and breathed into humanity the breath of divine life so

that we would the bearers of the image of God to the whole of creation, the "Imago Dei." This Divine creator is also the God who called forth Abraham the father of the people of Israel. This is the same God who spoke to Moses at the summit of Sinai in the midst of the holy fire and smoke of the divine glory, the Shekinah. This same God, whom the people of Israel worshiped in holy awe, is now revealed in the person of the Son, Jesus the Christ, to be a being of pure and Holy love. "God is Love." And as such this God , we are told, loved, and is loving continuously the world, the entire cosmos, the whole of the universe which is the masterpiece of the divine creator. We learn from the Torah that the whole of creation, both spirit and matter, was declared good by her creator from the very beginning. We now learn from Jesus that this same creation is the object of the Creator's love. It is revealed that the whole of the created world along with the human race, indeed, especially because of the human race, is the beloved of God. But in some mysterious way, for reasons we cannot fully comprehend, God's beloved creation became subject to death. The whole universe along with humanity, the divine image, became hostage to the entropy of corruption and mortality. "Death reigns." All things die, all things pass away. Everything perishes. The whole of the universe is disintegrating into oblivion. But this simple verse of the Gospel tells us that this God could not stand by and allow this to happen. "God so loved the world..." In the depths of the divine wisdom, Hagia Sophia, God determines the unfolding plan of His eternal will, and that divine plan was determined from the very foundation of the world. God would redeem the whole of creation and He would begin His redemptive work of love within the human race.

God would send the divine Son, the eternal Word, the Beloved One, into the created world to bring the message of the Gospel to humankind. This was done so that those human beings who would believe this Gospel and put their trust in the person of the Son, the Word made flesh, would once again have eternal life and would no longer be perishing, would no longer be subject to corruption at the hands of that grim reaper called the Death, ha Thanatos. Through this saving action of God in Christ death would be overcome. "The last enemy to be destroyed is Death." With this new life, given to us by grace and received in faith, we are now enabled to be agents of God's redeeming love in the world. We, the human race, now play an indispensable role in the salvation of the whole world. Salvation is not limited to a few human beings, but involves the entire universe. Salvation is not merely individual but it is cosmic, it is the saving act of God for the whole of His beloved creation. As human beings who's hearts have been transformed by the divine act of God in Jesus Christ, we become co-workers in the divine act of saving the world. We are to be beings filled and transformed by God into creatures of perfect and holy love. As such we are called to love all creation and we are to love everyone into becoming loving beings as well. We are to love a hostile universe into loving. Love is infectious and we are to become the agents of this infection of divine love. It is now through us that the redeeming love of God for the universe is brought to manifestation until that time when Christ's victory over all evil and death is fully manifested and then humanity in Christ will hand all things over to God "that God may be all in all." This is our eternal destiny.

No wonder poor Nicodemus was incredulous and at the same time was irresistibly drawn to this Gospel of which the person of Jesus was the embodiment in the temple of his body. This is why Nicodemus was there the day the broken and dead body of Jesus was taken down from the cross. This is why Nicodemus with tears in his eyes, tenderly washed the battered and bruised body of Jesus and along with Joseph of Arimathea, carefully wrapped the lifeless body of the Son of God and laid Him in a tomb. They left the tomb after sealing it shut with no idea of what universe shaking event was to take place in just three days time, the beginning of the new creation in a way they could have never imagined. This is the Story. This is the Gospel story that is summed up in the few simple words, "For God so loved the world..." We become a part of that larger story. The journey of Lent reminds us of that. During

Lent we make our way into the ultimate Love Story, the eternal story of God's love for the world. We do this every time we act in obedience to the love of God. For whenever we perform a loving act for another, especially for those who are at the bottom of human need, we have joined our stories to the Divine Story. Whenever we perform an act of love to an animal or plant, to the earth or any aspect of creation, we are living out the mystery of God's Love Story in the midst of our own personal story. That is what full redemption is all about. This is what Lent means to those who believe in the person and work of Jesus Christ.

The Anointed One and the Mass of Holy Chrism

. The Chrism Mass is an opportunity for all the faithful to share in the joy that these oils will bring: those who are sick, those who are preparing for baptism especially at Easter Vigil, and all those to be confirmed or ordained. Although we may not be present for each individual celebration of these sacraments, by participating in the Chrism Mass we share in the joy of those sacred moments because we know those oils will not remain in the bottles unused, but will be poured out again and again upon those in need. Every year we are reminded that Jesus of Nazareth is the Christ: the anointed One of God. Jesus, the Messiah, was sent to free God's people from the slavery of death. The Chrism Mass is a means to prepare for the annual celebration of the Paschal Mystery during the Triduum, the days from Holy Thursday to Easter Sunday. he Chrism Mass is an opportunity for all the faithful to share in the joy that these oils will bring: those who are sick, those who are preparing for baptism especially at Easter Vigil, and all those to be confirmed or ordained. Although we may not be present for each individual celebration of these sacraments, by participating in the Chrism Mass we share in the joy of those sacred moments because we know those oils will not remain in the bottles unused, but will be poured out again and again upon those in need. Every year we are reminded that Jesus of Nazareth is the Christ: the anointed One of God. Jesus, the Messiah, was sent to free God's people from the slavery of death. The Chrism Mass is a means to prepare for the annual celebration of the Paschal Mystery during the Triduum, the days from Holy Thursday to Easter Sunday. "

The Feast of Easter is the Feast of the Resurrection of Jesus Christ

On the first Sunday after the first full moon after the Spring equinox, Christians throughout the world will gather together in churches and cathedrals, in chapels and other sacred places, to pray, to remember, and to celebrate. We will gather at this time, as we have done year after year for nearly two millennia, to celebrate and proclaim the great mystery of our Christian Faith that, "Christ has died, Christ is risen, Christ will come again!"

At the very heart of our Christian spirituality and witness is the person of Jesus our Savior and the events associated with His life, death, and resurrection, which have become for us the means of our salvation and that of the whole world. His suffering and death culmination in His glorious resurrection and ascension into Heaven is the very center from which all the grace and hope of the Gospel message emanates.

From the very first generation of eyewitnesses until this present generation of ours, Christians have realized that, in some mysterious way, these events in life, death, and resurrection of Jesus of Nazareth in Jerusalem centuries ago have made salvation possible for all of humanity.

In carrying the cross, Jesus carried all of the fears and pain that burden our hearts. By embracing death, Jesus took hold of that which holds humanity most helpless. By rising from the dead, He opens the door to a new kind of life for humanity: an immortal life, a life not subject to death; a divine life, a life of endless possibility and creative potential; a grace-filled life, a life that is immersed in the greatest power in the universe, the irresistible power of divine love.

Through the gift of baptism we, in some mysterious way, participate in the saving event of Christ. In baptism we die with Christ. In baptism we are raised with Christ to a new, eternal, and spiritual life. Because of our participation through baptism in the death of Christ we possess that sure and certain hope of resurrection in the world to come. "In dying Jesus destroyed our death. In rising He restores our life," that is, the divine life that was always intended by God to be ours. This is the Paschal Mystery. Jesus died because humanity dies; humanity is raised to eternal life because Jesus was raised from the dead, never to die again.

Together, as Christian communities, we will renew and relive this great Paschal Mystery as we gather to proclaim the joyous news that Jesus has conquered death. Together we will celebrate the reality of our salvation through the blessing of fire, the lighting of the Paschal candle, the singing of the Exultet and the blessing of the baptismal waters. Once again, we shall together partake of the blessed sacrament of Christ's body and blood in our Eucharistic meal which we continuously celebrate until He comes again in glory for the final redemption of all the world.

Although we are separated from one another by many miles we remain joined together in the Spirit through our Ecumenical Catholic Communion as we gather this year in our various faith communities across the nation to observe Holy Week by remembering and reliving the great mystery of Christ's love that has become not only our salvation but the salvation of all the world.

Let us celebrate and rejoice on this most Holy Feast of Easter. Alleluia!

The Mystery of Faith and the Glory of Easter

"Dying you destroyed our death; Rising you restored our life, Lord Jesus, come in glory." Embodied in these words from the Holy Liturgy, in which the gathered community intones upon hearing the call of the deacon, "Let us proclaim the mystery of faith," is the very heart of the Christian experience. The Mystery of Faith, which we encounter in the very act of celebrating the Eucharist, is summed up in these very words which we sing or recite week after week at the table of Jesus Christ. This is the Paschal Mystery of Christ in which we participate every time we gather as the People of God to partake of the Eucharistic bread and wine that has become for us the body and blood of Christ, that is, the very life of Christ among us and then within us. This is the moment when our holy communion with God and one another is fully realized in the Risen Christ. It is the moment we recognize Christ is truly among us in the breaking of the bread and the sharing of the cup, his body broken, his blood poured out. It is a sacred moment when we glimpse the in-breaking of the "age to come" into the here and now of our lives in this present age of suffering and death which is already passing away as God's new creation is now coming into being in our very midst. The paschal Mystery of Christ is that decisive act of God in Christ that saves God's beloved humanity from the tyranny of death and sin. In some mysterious way that we cannot even begin to fully comprehend, the suffering and dying of Jesus sets us free from our complicity with evil, of which our many sins are but the evidence of humankinds' "yes" to the angelic lie of the evil one who has held us hostage throughout this present evil age. And by rising from the dead Jesus delivers the decisive and fatal blow to death itself. In so doing He restores to us the essence of life, which is His life in us.

We participate in this saving action of Christ by our baptism in the waters whereby we die with Christ in his death and are raised to new life in Christ through the gift of the Holy Spirit which is the divine guarantee to us that God will complete our salvation by the resurrection of our own bodies when this age finally passes away and we behold the New Heavens and the New Earth with the descent of the Holy City of the New Jerusalem coming down from out of heaven to rest upon the Earth in which God will dwell forever with the human race, the perfect consummation of the communion of heaven and earth, of divinity and humanity, the ultimate

divinization not only of the new humanity but of the whole universe. Salvation is inclusive of the entire cosmos not just a few million human souls. Our salvation is the coming of the new creation where all evil and the power of death will be no more. The thought of the coming of this new world, this new age, is incomprehensible to us for all we have ever known is this present existence. It is staggering to even try to imagine this new creation. And yet it remains our deepest hope and our greatest longing.

At Easter we celebrate anther part of this mystery, namely the resurrection of Christ from the dead. The resurrection is not merely God's validation of the person and work of His holy son, Jesus, but it is the very beginning of the new age. Christ becomes the first fruits of the new creation which now has already come upon us in him. This also marks the beginning of the end of the old creation that has been held in bondage to corruption and decay for countless millennia. Oh, my beloved sisters and brothers in Christ, this is the Mystery of Faith that we proclaim. It is this mystery which is already at work within us, and to which we are called to live out in the here and now of our lives. It is this mystery that enables us to become co-workers with Christ and one another in the ushering in of this new creation. We have become agents of God's light illuminating the darkness of the world through our faithful witness to this coming reality of God's reign and the ongoing work of bringing God's justice and peace to our broken and suffering world. This is the Mystery of Faith. It is the Gospel we proclaim. It is the witness we bear to the world concerning that mystery "which is Christ in you the hope of glory." So let us never cease in praying the words of this prayer, for in so doing we proclaim the glory of the Easter we celebrate: "Dying you destroyed our death; rising you restored our life; Lord Jesus, come in glory."

Pentecost: The Coming of the Holy Spirit

In the opening pages of the Book of Genesis we encounter the great song of creation in which we are told that the Divine Spirit hovered over the primordial waters from which God, by means of the Word, called forth the whole of creation. Through the activity and power of the Holy Spirit, the universe was born in all its entirety, complexity, and potentiality.

In the story of the Garden of Eden we are told that God formed humanity from the dust of the earth, and, by the breath (ruah) of the Holy Spirit, humanity became a living being in the image of God. Somehow, however, humanity, along with the whole of creation, became alienated from God; we lost the Divine Spirit. We were made subject to the reign of death.

Nonetheless, God did not abandon us. By the power and inspiration of the Holy Spirit, God was revealed to us through the words of the ancient Hebrew prophets. God's self-disclosure to humanity in the prophetic word was for the purpose of calling humanity back into relationship with the Divine, which is the life of the Spirit.

Through the power of the Holy Spirit, the Blessed Virgin Mary conceived within her womb the Savior of the world who would be called the Son of God. When Jesus was baptized by John in the waters of the Jordan River, the Holy Spirit descended from Heaven and anointed Him to become our Messiah, the Christ, who, through His death and resurrection, would bring salvation to all of the world. Having been anointed by the Holy Spirit, Jesus was able to proclaim the Gospel of the Kingdom of God in Divine power. Through the Spirit He healed the sick, expelled the demonic, gave sight to the blind, and raised the dead. After dying on the cross and being buried in the tomb, we are told that it was through the power of the Holy Spirit that Jesus was raised from the dead. Because of the resurrection of Christ, the Holy Spirit is now made available to us. It began in this way:

Before ascending into Heaven, Jesus instructed His disciples to remain in Jerusalem to await "the promise of the Father"; that is, the gift of the Holy Spirit. With the coming of the Holy Spirit on the day of Pentecost, the disciples received the same Divine power that Jesus had to continue the proclamation of the Gospel and the saving work that He had begun. With the arrival of Pentecost came the long-awaited day in which the Holy Spirit would be restored to humanity and ultimately to all creation. That same Spirit has been given to us

through the waters of baptism. That same Spirit is at work in all of our hearts and lives and is our guarantee of eternal life in God's kingdom yet to come.

This Pentecost, let us open our hearts so that our lives may be filled with the Holy Spirit and that we would become a people of the Spirit living in the same joy and power of Jesus and His first disciples.

For it is through the gift of the Holy Spirit that we are able to fully realize the life of Christ in us, a life of faith, hope and love.

Let us celebrate and rejoice in gratitude for the gift of the Holy Spirit in our lives!

Ministry Contact Information

Saint Matthew Ecumenical Catholic Church
1111 W. Town & Country Rd
Orange, CA 92868

Website Address:
www.saint-matthew.org

www.ingramcontent.com/pod-product-compliance
Lightning Source LLC
LaVergne TN
LVHW021401080426
835508LV00020B/2394